REPRINTS OF ECONOMIC CLASSICS

# *The Effects of Civilization*

# *THE*
# EFFECTS OF CIVILIZATION
## *ON THE PEOPLE*
## In European States

*BY*

CHARLES HALL

*With:* *OBSERVATIONS on the PRINCIPAL CONCLUSION in MR. MALTHUS'S ESSAY on POPULATION*

[1805]

REPRINTS OF ECONOMIC CLASSICS

*Augustus M. Kelley, Bookseller*
*New York 1965*

*Library of Congress Catalogue Card Number*
*65 - 19643*

PRINTED IN THE UNITED STATES OF AMERICA
*by* SENTRY PRESS, NEW YORK, N. Y. 10019

THE

# EFFECTS OF CIVILIZATION

ON

# THE PEOPLE

IN

# EUROPEAN STATES

*BY CHARLES HALL, M. D.*

*LONDON:*

PRINTED FOR THE AUTHOR,

AND SOLD BY T. OSTELL, 3, AVEMARIA-LANE, AND C. CHAPPEL, PALL-MALL.

1805.

# PREFACE

It may appear to many that a man, who has been employed during his whole life in the study and practice of medicine, cannot be a fit person to write on a subject of a political nature: to such people the following considerations are submitted:—

That the Essay treats on the Effects of Civilization on the mass of the people.

That the principal effect of civilization is the reduction of the mass of the people in civilized societies to their present condition.

Of this condition, *i. e.* the manner in which the people live, who has more opportunities of acquiring the knowledge than a Physician? He is admitted into the dwellings of all ranks of people, and into the innermost parts of them: he sees them

by

by their fire-side, at their tables, and in their beds: he sees them at work, and at their recreations: he sees them in health, in sickness, and in the article of death: he is frequently made acquainted with their hopes and their fears, their successes and their disappointments, as these have often a relation to their diseases; and, possessing their confidence, they also frequently unbosom themselves to him on matters not connected with the state of their healths. The physician therefore is put in possession of more facts with respect to the condition of the people than any other person; and it is only from the collection of such facts that we can arrive at the knowledge of the causes of them; for the investigation of which his education peculiarly fits him.

For all these reasons, it seems, a physician is the most proper person to treat on the subject of the following discourse.

Tavistock,
April 30, 1808.

# CONTENTS.

XXXV. Whether

THE

# EFFECTS OF CIVILIZATION

ON THE

*MASS OF THE PEOPLE.*

## SECTION I.

### DEFINITION OF CIVILIZATION.

WE understand by civilization that manner of living in societies of men, which is opposite to that of those who are called savages; such as are the natives of North America, &c.

It consists in the study and knowledge of the sciences, and in the production and enjoyment of the conveniences, elegancies, and luxuries of life.

It does not seem to arise from any particular constitution of governments, or to be attributable to the administration of them, but to flow from the natural propensities of mankind.

SEC-

## SECTION II.

### DIVISION OF THE PEOPLE INTO TWO ORDERS.

If a native of North America were to come to some European nation, he would probably, after having informed himself of the different states and conditions of the people in this society, be most struck with the great profusion and splendor of some among them, and the penury and obscurity of all the others ; and, in this, it would appear to him, that this civilized people differed most from those of his own country, where the condition of all is the same. He would naturally, therefore, divide the people, whose situation he had so observed, into two orders, viz. the rich and the poor. We shall make the same division ; and, as the different conditions of the people are among the greatest effects of civilization, shall inquire into the situation of each of these orders separately.

We often hear of inquiries into the state of nations being made in legislative assem-

assemblies; but such inquiries are of a very confined nature. If made by a minister of state, nothing is understood further than the financial state of a kingdom, the supplies and expenditure: if by a secretary at war, the state of the army is the object of inquiry: if by a merchant, the state of trade and commerce. But it seems that there is a subject of much more importance than any of these to a nation, that never enters into the thoughts of any one to make inquiries about; namely, the state and condition of the great mass of the people: how they are fed; how they are clothed; what kind of houses they live in; how they are supplied with fuel; how they are instructed; in short, what advantages, corporeal, mental, and even spiritual, they enjoy or are deprived of. To know these particulars with regard to the poor, that is, the great mass of the people, is truly to know the state of a nation.

The people in a civilized state may be divided into many different orders; but, for the purpose of investigating the manner in which they enjoy or are deprived

of

of the requisites to support the health of their bodies and minds, they need only be divided into two classes, viz. the rich and the poor, as we have before done: for, people in the same circumstances as to property enjoy the same advantages in those respects, whether the means of placing them in those circumstances are derived from landed estates, benefices of the church, the practice of the law, or any other profession or trade.

---

## SECTION III.

### THAT THE POOR ARE NOT SUFFICIENTLY SUPPLIED WITH THE NECESSARIES OF LIFE.

We will begin with the poor, they being by far the greater number of the people in most civilized countries; and, therefore, whatever regards them should be deemed of the greater importance.

And first, as to their food. The food of man is of a mixed nature, partly animal,

mal, partly vegetable. A certain proportion of the former is necessary to the health, strength, and growth of the human species, and without it those things cannot be obtained. The appetites and the organs he is furnished with by nature plainly indicate this.

It would be difficult to discover whether the poor have a sufficiency of animal and vegetable food, by any other method than by considering the quantity of each sort which their nature requires; and their means of obtaining that quantity; or, in other words, what their earnings are, and what quantity of food such earnings could procure.

The number of husbandmen in most states is greater probably than that of any class of artificers. To begin therefore with them. The average wages of a labourer appear to have been about eight shillings a week, previous to the few late years, more or less, according to the price of provisions in different nations. We will suppose that this labourer has a wife and three children. The wife, if she keeps the house clean, free from vermin, washes,

makes

makes and mends the husband's and children's clothes, dresses their victuals, &c. will not, or ought not to have any time to add any thing to the earnings of the husband. But we will suppose that she does, to the amount of two shillings per week; which makes their income ten shillings a week.

Whether ten shillings a week will furnish a proper quantity of flesh-meat, bread, flour, milk, butter, cheese, and clothes, bedding, fuel, soap, candles, salt, &c. I will leave to the reader to form his own conjectures on; for calculations made in this matter must be in a great measure arbitrary, and of course unsatisfactory. I shall only observe, that Judge Hale, above a century ago, after having made a more diligent inquiry than any body else seems to have done, judged ten shillings a week as little as a family could be supported on in England at that time, at the price things then were.

But I think a general argument may be adduced, that will throw great light on this matter; and but too clearly show that that sum is inadequate, and that

it

it was so at the time mentioned; and that the poor are not in fact furnished with the requisite quantity of the necessaries of life. This argument is of the presumptive kind, but that is the only sort the nature of the subject will admit of.

If we consider the œconomy of nature with regard to animal and vegetable life, we may observe that, in order, probably, to keep up the different species of living creatures and plants, the seed produced of both kinds is very abundant; for instance, the spawn of a carp or a salmon shall amount to eighty or a hundred thousand; insomuch that any one species of fish would in a few ages fill the ocean, if all that were brought into life were brought to maturity. In the same manner the offspring of any one species of land animal would fill, some in a longer, others in a shorter time, the whole earth, if proper and sufficient sustenance were provided for them. The same may be said of any vegetable, if the ground were prepared for the reception of its seed, and the other plants destroyed to make room

for

for it. To illustrate this; if the number of rabbits put into a warren to stock it, be less than the quantity which the ground will maintain, they will increase till they rise to the utmost number that it will maintain; but if the number which it at first was stocked with be greater than it will carry, they will gradually sink down to that number. Again, if you plant a piece of ground with young trees much thicker than they ought to be, so many will die away after some years, that they will be reduced to that number which ought in the first instance to have been planted; the stronger plants, after a long contest, destroying the weaker. So that the increase in the number of animals of any particular species does not depend so much on the number of their young brought into existence, as on the degree of the support and sustenance they receive, after being brought into life, to preserve them and bring them to maturity. Hence we certainly conclude, if the number of individuals of any species of animals do not increase in proportion to the number brought into life, that it

is

is owing to the offspring of them not being properly sustained.

These facts obtain, with regard to the human race, in as full a manner as in the brute species, or in the class of vegetables.

We find that the inhabitants in few of the states of Europe have doubled in five hundred years. Hence there is a presumption that the people have not been well fed, or have wanted some other thing necessary to their subsistence; for, where their subsistence is better, we see they actually increase much faster.

In America, the land is not engrossed by a few, in the manner it is in Europe. It is easy there for a man to procure ground sufficient to produce what nature requires for the preservation and health of his offspring: the consequence is, that the inhabitants increase much faster than they do in Europe; some states doubling every fourteen years, others every twenty years. This happy effect may in part be owing to their being exempted from the many destructive employments to which most Europeans are subjected to: but, whichever

whichever of those ways it be, it is still to be ascribed to their not being arrived at the state of extreme civilization.

We do not suppose that even this, the greatest increase that happens in America, is the greatest possible; or that it is so great as would actually be, if the people and their offspring were well supplied with every thing nature requires; since in America, on account of the great labour in clearing the ground for cultivation, the quantity tilled by the first planters may frequently be too scanty. But if any European state, consisting of ten millions, were to increase in the proportion they do in America, viz. to double in twenty years, they would increase ten millions in every twenty years; that is, five hundred thousand a year. Hence, therefore, in such a case, this number fall a sacrifice every year to the want of proper or sufficient food and other necessaries; the unwholesomeness of their employments; or to some other cause equally attributable to extreme civilization. A sad reflection this! It is nevertheless strictly true, or very near the truth: a loss greater than the most destructive wars have ever occasioned*.

Another fact strengthens this argument. When the Equitable Insurance Office at Blackfriars Bridge was first established, the premiums taken were according to a ratio proposed by Dr. Price, who formed it from the accounts of the annual deaths taken from the bills of mortality kept in different cities of Europe. These deaths were about one in twenty-two, annually, of all the people, taken indiscriminately. Proceeding thus, the profits of the Society were so great, that in a few years they realized their enormous capital; upon which, their premiums were lowered. Their profits being still very great, they returned, in a very honourable manner, part of the premiums that had been received from the insured, which they continue to do, at certain periods, with still greater liberality. The Society,

* The Chinese, who suffer the exposition of their children, and even appoint men to destroy them, seem to act more humanely than the Europeans, who cause the long languishing sufferings of their children.

notwith-

notwithstanding, continues to increase greatly in riches. The cause of this phœnomenon, therefore, was a matter of inquiry; on which it was found that they had adapted their premiums to the deaths of the rich and poor taken together; and it soon occurred that none but the rich were insured. Their extraordinary profit, therefore, must arise from the circumstance of there being fewer deaths annually among the rich than among the poor, in proportion to the numbers of both.

It is not possible to calculate what this great disproportion is between the deaths of the rich and the poor, as that cannot be done without the knowledge of the exact profits of the Company; but it seems probable, that the deaths of the poor are to those of the rich as two to one, in proportion to the numbers of each.

This greater mortality among the poor, can only be owing to the difference in the manner in which they are supplied with the necessaries of life.

I will add one other relation of a fact, from which the inference is obvious.

There

There are, at the cotton-mills belonging to Mr. Dale, of Lanark, in Scotland, three thousand children; these children are said to be treated in a proper manner, in most respects; the consequence is, that during a term of twelve years, viz. from 1785 to 1797, only fourteen have died*

This mortality is chiefly observable among children, of whom more than one half die before they are two years and a half old. Children, as well as the young of all animals, bear want and hardships worse than adult persons, and full-grown brute animals. Infants, though their deaths be really occasioned by the above-mentioned causes, have nearly the same symptoms that occur in many chronic diseases; to which their deaths are frequently attributed.

The diseases which are the chief agents in this great mortality among infants, are fevers and the disorders of the stomach and bowels. The latter are so frequent among infants, that physicians, when

* James Neel's Letter to Dr. Lettsom. Gent. Mag for June 1804.

called

called to them, almost always consider these as the seat of the complaint. The weaknesses or disorder of the bowels seem chiefly to be occasioned by the poor, watery, meagre vegetable diet of the children and of their mothers. The latter, from the use of this diet, have their milk poor and not sufficiently animalised. To produce good milk, the woman should be well fed with a full proportion of animal food; perhaps some quantity of good beer; live in good houses; good air; be employed in wholesome and pleasant exercises; and void of care. The children, after they are weaned, should have a sufficiency of well-prepared vegetable and animal food, such as new milk, and broths of fresh meat: for want of these the state of their bowels is induced, which proves so destructive to our race. With regard to the fevers of children, there are many of them generated by the circumstances of their condition; almost all of them are exasperated by it. It has frequently happened to me, and to all other physicians, that, after being called to a child of a man of fortune, ill of this disease, whom I have found in a large lofty

room,

room, well ventilated, clean and sweet; bed soft, undisturbed by noise, anxiously attended by people relieving each other; furnished with every thing the cellars, the kitchen, the garden, the druggist, can furnish; in short, every thing the four quarters of the world can supply: after, I say, being with such a patient, we are frequently entreated to visit the child or children of a poor man, in the same illness; several of them generally lying in the same bed; heated by and heating each other, in a small room, corrupted by the exhalations of the whole family; disturbed by one another's cries; their wakefulness and restlessnes, the effects of the disorder, increased by the vermin and hard beds, covered by filthy clothes; having nothing proper to use from the cellar, the kitchen, the garden, or apothecary's shop; no attendants but the poor mother, worn out by watchings, anxiety, &c.; the father from home, obliged to leave it to get their daily bread. That these things happen unavoidably in almost all cases, in poor families, all medical people must bear testimony; and also to the ill effects of them

them on the sufferers. I have said unavoidably, which is true; for, though single instances by charitable assistance may in some things be relieved, it is impossible that in general the poor can be better supplied; unless you alter the condition of the whole, by giving them good houses, containing more and better rooms; better furniture; better linen; better supplies; in short, making their condition nearer to the first described; that is, wholly altering the condition of that whole order of people.

It is remarkable, that poor living does not lessen the fertility of women, though it deprives them of the means of bringing up their children. Adam Smith says, that it is not uncommon in the Highlands of Scotland for a woman to bear twenty children, and not to rear one of them. He adds, that officers of great experience have assured him, that, so far from recruiting their regiment, they have never been able to supply it with fifes and drums from all the soldiers' children that were born in it.

This slow increase of the people may be supposed by some to be not wholly attributable

butable to the difficulties attending the rearing of the children of the poor, and consequent mortality; and that it might be in part owing to these difficulties being foreseen and dreaded, by the more prudent part of the poor; and their being, from that consideration, prevented from marrying. This, no doubt, may happen sometimes; but prudence is not the virtue of the youthful, especially when opposed by a passion the strongest and most difficult to be checked that human nature is subject to. We are not warranted by any direct facts to ascribe much to this cause. When the masters of sheep-flocks are short of keep, from backward springs, poor land, or other causes; when the milk of the ewes is in small quantities, and a great loss of lambs follows; do they impute the slow increase of their flock to the ewes not taking the ram? The other cause of the slow increase of the people is more obvious. We see half of the children born, die before they are two years and a half old; and a very great part of the remainder drop off before they are seven. We have therefore no occasion to look for other causes. The

The Earl of Lauderdale, in a very ingenious discourse, lately published, on Wealth, quotes a passage from a letter of the Marquise of ——:

" On a soin de les marier d'ausi bonne " heure que les grands seigneurs, le pays " n'en est pas plus peuplé, car presque " tous les enfans meurent: les femmes n'y " ont presque pars de lait *."

But if three-fourths or two-thirds of this deficiency in the increase of the people be chargeable on the mortality complained of, we have still enough to lament. And it may be added, that if this forbearance of the poor, in the indulgence of their strongest desires, actually takes place, it strongly evinces the reality and magnitude of the evils they see around them.

What renders this matter still more grievous is, that there are many more sufferers than those who die, from the same causes: many who have struggled with the difficulties, and escaped with their lives, have suffered greatly in the conflict, and continue ever after to suffer

* Extrait d'une Lettre de la Marquise de * * A. M. * Du 17 Août 1767. Append. No. XIV.

from

from the injury their constitution received. As a proof of this, what rickety, squalid, dwarfed, distorted objects, do we see in the manufacturing towns of Europe! This will further appear from the consideration of the employments of the poor *.

## SECTION IV

### THE EMPLOYMENTS OF THE POOR INJURIOUS TO HEALTH.

THE employments of manufacturers are all injurious to the health of the body, and the improvement of the mind. These pernicious effects arise from,

1st, The sedentary nature of them, by which the necessary action and exercise of the body are prevented.

2dly, From the forced and unnatural postures of the body required in many trades, by which the functions of the body necessary to life and health are impeded.

* Vide Notes A. B. C. D. E. F.

3dly, From these being carried on in confined, unwholesome atmospheres, rendered nauseous and putrid from the filth of the rooms, and from the exhalations of their own bodies; as well as from the effluvia of the substances they work on, as oils, sizes, mercury, lead, paint; damps and noxious air in mines, &c. all add hurtful qualities to the air. Under the same head may be placed the excessive heat in glass-houses, smelting-houses, founderies, &c.

From one or other of these disadvantages there is scarcely any trade exempt, and hardly any individual of any trade that is not more or less affected by them. The sedentary kind appears to be least prejudical; but what a number of pale, languid, dropsical objects there are among women who make bone-lace, those are witnesses to, who have seen the many thousands of such in those places where it is manufactured.

The infinite number of trades into which these noxious employments branch out may be seen in the back streets of great cities and manufacturing towns, as also

may

may the many wretched objects there produced by them.

This general account will render it evident, to persons of reflection, what great devastations are made by the manufactures on the human species; it is therefore needless to enumerate the particular diseases they occasion. I cannot help, however, observing, that there is a great multiplicity of trades in which mercury is made use of: in some of these the workmen's lives are measured with great exactness; after suffering excruciating torments, they die, with great punctuality, in a year and half.

Nor can I forget mentioning the poor chimney-boy, who, after suffering inconceivable hardships, dies frequently, at length, of a disease attended with the most acute of all pains,—the cancer.

## SECTION V

### THEIR MINDS UNCULTIVATED.

HOWEVER ill-furnished the poor are in most civilized countries, in respect to sustenance, clothing, &c. they are still more neglected with regard to their minds; they indeed are excluded from all kind of improvement of their mental faculties. It is even by many supposed that all such knowledge would be prejudicial to them; that is, as they are to be worked as irrational animals, there is no reason why their rational faculties should be cultivated. And, indeed, if this their situation were necessarily such, and were unavoidable, and if it were not such through our injustice and cruelty to them, our fellow-creatures, and were such as could admit of no alteration or amendment, it would in that case perhaps be better that they should be brought up in ignorance, as they are; since they would, by any degree of knowledge, see more clearly, and feel more

more acutely, what they suffer, and the want of the comforts and happiness of which they are deprived. If they remain for ever the mere carriers of wood and water, they cannot certainly be kept too ignorant. But these poor wretches, I think, have a right, before they give up all the advantages of rational creatures, to expect a better reason for it, than that those things always were so. They have a right to expect that so great a difference in their lot and condition should not be made, unless indicated by nature itself, and made evident by its having refused them the faculties and powers for the acquisition of knowledge.

There are two methods of acquiring knowledge: the one, by thinking or meditation; that is, by the operations of our own minds within themselves: the other, by informing ourselves of the knowledge already acquired by others, which is done by books or living masters. Both of these methods the commonalty are debarred from. One should have thought the former might have been allowed them: that is not, however, the case; for to do that requires leisure, which is refused the poor man. Leisure in a poor man is thought quite a different thing from what it is to a rich man, and goes by a different name. In the poor, it is called idleness, the cause of all mischief. If it is so, why is it so? Because they have been, by this cruel system, deprived of opportunities of acquiring such rudiments as would qualify them for further attainments; that is to say, they are not to have leisure, because they have never had any to fit them to improve by such leisure. Most part of the manufacturing trades just occupy the mind so as to exclude all other ideas on which it might operate.

In the progress of the division of labour, the employment "of the far greater part "of those who live by labour, that is, the "great body of the people, comes to be "confined to a very few simple operations; "frequently to one or two. But the understandings of the greater part of men "are necessarily formed by their ordinary "employments. The man whose whole "life is spent in performing a few simple "operations, of which the effects too are "perhaps

" perhaps always the same, or very nearly " the same, has no occasion to exert his " understanding, or to exercise his inven- " tion, in finding out expedients for " removing difficulties which never occur. " He naturally loses, therefore, the habit " of such exertion, and generally becomes " as stupid and ignorant as it is possible " for human nature to become. The tor- " por of his mind renders him not only " incapable of relishing or bearing part in " any rational conversation, but of con- " ceiving any generous, noble, or tender " sentiment, and consequently of form- " ing any just judgment concerning many " even of the ordinary duties of life.

" It is otherwise in the barbarous socie- " ties, as they are called, of hunters, shep- " herds, or even of husbandmen in that " rude state of husbandry which precedes " the improvement of manufactures and " the extension of foreign commerce. In " such societies the varied occupations of " every man oblige every man to exert his " capacity, and to invent expedients for " removing difficulties which are continu- " ally occurring. Invention is kept alive,

" and

" and the mind is not suffered to fall into " that drowsy stupidity, which in a civi-" lized society seems to benumb the un-" derstanding of almost all the inferior " ranks of the people."—Adam Smith, vol. iii. p. 183.

---

## SECTION VI.

### THEIR MORAL AND SPIRITUAL INSTRUCTION NEGLECTED.

We have seen how manufactures tend to the utter exclusion of all rational improvement of the mind. We may further observe, that they generally tend to the prevention of moral and spiritual improvement. To speak first as to the latter; though perhaps it might be deemed presumptuous in me to say any thing on that subject.

The proof of the Christian system is founded on historical facts; from thence are

are drawn the principal motives of credibility, as they are called. We give credit to facts recorded in history, when they are related by an historian of credit; when other historians agree with him; and from the concurrence of other circumstances. But what idea has a totally ignorant man of the weight of the concurrence of historians, or the coincidence of facts? or what knowledge of history at all? certainly none. Hence, being deprived of the belief, he of course is deprived of all the other advantages of religion.

With respect to morals: Civilization has a twofold effect on the morals of the people; first, by depriving them of their original share of things, and reducing them to a state of both comparative and absolute poverty, it subjects them to more and much stronger temptations. Secondly, by their extreme ignorance, and little sense of religion in consequence of it, they are deprived of the strongest motives to resist them. Thus, all their temptations rendered stronger, their powers of resistance weaker, they could not

be

be expected to be different from what we find them.*

## SECTION VII.

### CONDITION OF THE POOR NOT HAPPY.

AUTHORS and preachers frequently inculcate to the poor, in their writings and sermons, contentment, and submission to the dispensations of Providence; such they pretend their hardships and depressed state to be; thus attributing the works of man to the beneficent Creator. They assert that the measure of happiness is much the same in all conditions, and nearly equal. Not to mention that such doctrine as this would suit every kind of oppression and tyranny, I believe it contrary

* To suffer the lower orders of the people to be ill-educated, to be totally inattentive to those wise regulations of state policy which might serve to guard and improve their morals, and then to punish them for crimes which originated from bad habits, has the appearance of a cruelty not less severe than any which is exercised under the most despotic government.—*Treatise on Police*, &c. by P. COLQUHOUN, LL.D.

contrary to fact, and that from considerations drawn from the constitution of the human frame.* I shall say nothing as to the destitute condition of their minds, which must deprive them of every consolation from thence. The sensations and feelings of their bodies must subject them to correspondent ones of the mind, and rob them of such satisfaction as it is asserted they do enjoy.

Physicians know that there is a great degree of sympathy existing between the body and the mind; that they mutually affect each other; that the stomach is the principal medium of their reciprocal feelings; that when the sensations of this organ are comfortable, the mind is in an easy and pleasant state. A poor watery vegetable diet has the effect of exciting contrary feelings in the stomach, which are communicated to the mind: hence, it is depressed and anxious; hence, poor men generally have recourse to tobacco, which, being of a narcotic nature, deadens the sensations, and relieves the un-

* An old author says—Οὐδὲν πενίας βαρύτερόν ἐστιν φορτίον.

easiness both of the stomach, and of the mind depending on it: for which reason, we see they would rather go without their food than their tobacco. Numbers of them fly to the use of spirituous liquors, which is the remedy precisely adapted to their case; and it is to be wondered at that drunkenness is not more frequent among them than it is.* But besides the uneasinesses occasioned by those sensations, can they see with indifference their offspring perishing for the want of such things as they perceive around them, but which they cannot reach? † Can they see without pain the luxurious abundance of the rich, and compare it with their own pinching poverty? To write or preach in this manner, is adding insult to oppression.

I have now stated briefly and generally, the situation of the poor in most European nations, with regard to the necessaries of life, their employments, and

* A dejection of spirits will rob the poor husbandman of the ease and comfort which he should feel when the labour of the day is ended. HEBERDEN's *Comment*. *p*. 220.

† Αγορὰν ἰδεῖν ἔυοψον, ἰυπορȣ̃ντι μεν
Ἥδιστον· ἂν δε ἀπορῆ τισ ἀθλιώτατον.

their

their moral and spiritual instruction ; and I have avoided entering into the description of the particular hardships, diseases, and instances of mortality, which so much abound in it, these being too obvious and affecting to need a representation to people of any observation, and endued with any sensibility; and, besides, my intention is rather to find out the causes of, and, if possible, a remedy, for the evils, than to give a laboured description of them. I shall first endeavour to discover the cause of their want of a sufficient quantity of the necessaries of life.

---

## SECTION VIII.

### THE CAUSE OF THE SCARCITY OF THE NECESSARIES OF LIFE.

Before I enter on the causes of the scarcity of the necessaries of life in general, I shall premise a few words relating particularly to the great scarcity that lately prevailed for two or three seasons, in a great part of Europe. Many people were of opinion, that the real scarcity of provisions was not proportionable to the high price they bore, but that this was occasioned by artificial causes, and several were assigned of that kind: the wealth of great farmers, and the assistance of bankers given to lesser ones, have, in some people's opinions, enabled both to keep their corn, and such other things as their farms produce, from market; and by these means to raise the price of them. Jobbers, regraters, and millers, are charged with occasioning the same effect. Not to observe that such people are not new, and have subsisted a long time without such an effect to all these supposed causes, and such as these, one common and short answer may be given. That as the price was near four times the usual one, the poor could not with their earnings buy more than a third or fourth part of what they used to buy when it was lower; consequently they must consume less. Therefore if the quantity of corn in the country was not small in proportion to this diminished consumption, there would be,

towards

towards harvest, a great deal of corn remaining in the hands of the farmers: which the farmers would, if they considered their own interest, then bring to market in greater quantities than they had done before; for they must suppose that, after harvest, the price would fall, and, consequently, that they should be great losers. But, if they had brought it to market in abundance at the latter end of the summer, the price must have fallen: or, if they had not brought it to market in that manner, there must have been a great deal of old corn in their hands after the harvest; which, if you suppose them to have been so unwise as to suffer, still this must have appeared since. Whatever doubt, therefore, there might have been in the beginning of the summer*, with respect to the cause of the high price, there can be none now; time having, on this occasion, as in most others, discovered the truth, that the dearness was owing to real scarcity.

What, then, is the cause of this great evil so often recurring; and in every season,

* of 1801.

when

when the corn crops are not abundant, so afflicting to the great majority of the people of almost all civilized states?

The scarcity or abundance of the produce of the earth, are the effects of causes both physical and moral.

The physical cause of the production of the necessaries of life, is the property of the earth to produce them, or, in other words, the natural fertility of the soil.

The effects of this power of the earth, though uniformly acting, or disposed to act, are increased or diminished by two causes, to wit; the greater or less quantity of the labour of man bestowed on it, and the favourableness or unfavourableness of seasons.

The quantity of man's labour applied being much the same one year as another, we might suppose that the quantity of the produce of the land would be uniform, and differing but little in different years.

The difference in the quantity of the produce of the necessaries of life in one year, from that of other years, must depend on the difference of seasons.

But whether or not the general produce,

i. e. that of a number of years taken together, of the necessaries of life, be proportioned to the number of people inhabiting a country, depends on the qnantity of land they occupy, and on the number of hands employed in cultivating it.

That the quantity of land inhabited by a people is too little, I believe does not happen in any instance; but that too few hands are employed, in almost all instances, in civilized countries.

The natural or spontaneous produce of the soil, or the produce of the soil unassisted, however fertile, will not be sufficient for the sustenance of nearly the number of people that inhabit any civilized part of it. In those parts of America which are not inhabited by Europeans, the spontaneous produce of the earth, with very little assistance from cultivation, is sufficient for the whole support of the inhabitants; but then these are very few in number, in comparison to the exte ntof the country they occupy. To support great numbers, the land must be cultivated; and the quantity of the produce of it will be, the degree of fertility of it being given, as the

the number of hands or the quantity of labour bestowed on it. If reduced to a state of pasture, it will produce more food for man than if covered with trees, or in the state of a forest. Again, this produce will be inferior to that of arable lands; and this again to that of land managed as in a garden. In these different modes of cultivation, namely, pasture, agriculture, and horticulture, the produce rises in quantity in the order in which they are here set down; or as the number of hands employed. This therefore being the case, it is obvious that to produce plenty it requires, besides fertile land and good seasons, the employing a sufficient number of hands on the land. It will be shown, hereafter, that not only in years of scanty crops, but that in all years, the produce of the land is insufficient for the inhabitants, in all or nearly all the civilized countries; and that, therefore, when a scarce year happens, they experience great distress. We have now, I think, ascertained the real cause of scarcity, to wit, that a sufficient number of hands are not employed on the land. We are next to inquire, what is the

cause

cause of this want of hands in agriculture. This cause must be of a moral nature.

For the present purpose, the people which compose a civilized nation may be divided into three sorts: the first, consisting of those who work in cultivating the land; the second, of those who are employed in trade and manufactures; the third, of those who do nothing. The first sort, it is obvious, furnishes the provisions for itself and the other two; and the whole will be furnished, either scantily or plentifully, as the first sort bears the greater or less proportion to it *. Notwithstanding this is sufficiently evident, and that bread can only be supplied by the husbandman, and that plenty of it can only be supplied by a sufficient number of them: yet it is trade and manufactures that are said to give bread to people, and to be what ought chiefly to be relied on for their sustenance; but this can only be true when the articles got up by them are sent to other countries, and the produce of them there laid out in the necessaries of life, and brought back for the support

* This proportion is as one to six nearly, at present.

of

of those employed in getting them up. It is known that this is never the case, except in great scarcities, when it always proves very inadequate; no importation having exceeded one-sixth part of the consumption.

The manufactures, in which the great majority of the labouring hands in many nations are employed, are of various kinds: they may be divided, however, into two, viz. such as are of the grosser kind, and are of prime and general use in life; and such others as are more refined and in use only by the rich, are not of prime necessity, but may be dispensed with. It seems natural to suppose that these latter should have only such a number of hands in them as could well be spared, and that a sufficient number should be reserved to produce an abundance of such things as are more useful, and of greater necessity. This, notwithstanding, is not the fact, as appears by the frequent recurrence of great scarcity in less abundant seasons; and its prevailing in some degree, as will be shown hereafter, in all seasons. We must therefore inquire into the

the cause that prevents the proper number of hands from being employed in raising that which is most necessary to the existence of all the people, and directs them to the production of such things as are enjoyed only by the few, and by them may be easily dispensed with. This cause, whatever it be, must be a very powerful one, since it turns things from the course to which they are naturally and strongly inclined.

The cause that can divert the labour of the people of most civilized countries from such occupations as have such an evident and direct tendency to produce for themselves the necessaries and comforts of life, and direct it to others which have not that obvious tendency, may be threefold; 1st, optional; 2d, delusive; 3d, compulsive.

As to the first, it has been remarked, that nations in their progress from a savage to a civilized state, have shown a great reluctance to quit the employment of their *former* state, namely, that of hunting, which is probably natural to man, he being of the carnivorous species of animals, and consequently that of prey; and hunting is nothing

thing but the mode or act of taking prey. The life of hunters consists in reverses either of violent exercise or total inaction; neither of which fits them for the confinement and long continued labour of manufactures which, therefore, they have always showed an aversion from; and it is a long time, even where they have the advantages of it before their eyes, in the practice of neighbouring Europeans, before they confine themselves to the regular and laborious occupations of agriculture. During many of the first ages, even of the most polished states, the business of agriculture was left to the slaves; the freemen enjoying their liberty in the sports of the field, or in the camp. This was the case in Sparta, where the Helotes performed the business of tilling the earth. And after man had arrived, as in Rome, at a state of civilization, in which the labour of the field was become tolerable, and held honourable, the arts and manufactures were thrown upon the slaves, and practised by them only: and it is not to be wondered at, since the works of manufactures, though so many and various in trading nations, are

are all of them, as has been observed before, carried on within doors, in confined rooms, shutting out the pleasant objects of nature, frequently within frames like cages, in offensive atmospheres, generally rendered more nauseous by the effluvia of the subject worked on, always by that of the bodies and filthy clothes of the workmen; their postures bent, doubled, and every way distorted. Add to this, the tendency of them, so injurious and destructive to their health and lives. It seems, therefore, that it was never through choice that manufactures were entered into by any people; it must, therefore, be from one or both of the other causes, viz. delusion or compulsion.

By the laws of most civilized nations, no man is compelled to work at any particular trade or manufacture; but at some trade or other, every one who has no property must work: and as the employment of the husbandmen is limited to such a number as the capital of farmers enables them to employ, all above that number must betake themselves to other kinds of employments; and from circumstances attending

attending each person, that person is determined to such or such a trade, which it is next to impossible for him to avoid. A tailor more easily brings up his son to be a tailor than he can to be a mason. A fisherman more easily makes his son a fisherman or a sailor, than of any other trade. Thus, with regard to the father, it was hardly optional; but, with regard to the son, altogether out of his power to make any choice in the matter.

If a poor man is employed by a master, and is paid by him the price of his hire, no injury is supposed to be done; on the contrary, it is thought that the finding employment for the labourer is beneficial to the individual as well as the public. But this is true only in a very limited sense. To be of service to the public, and indeed to the labourer, the product of the labour ought to be of such a kind as to be useful, and to consist of something that contributes to supply the wants of mankind. If a man, for instance, is employed in removing a heap of stones from one place to another, and from thence back again, and so repeatedly; if he is paid for so doing,

doing, where is the harm, it is said. The harm would be evident if a greater number were employed in that way; or, if the whole of the people were so for some time, we should then be destitute of the necessaries of life. Hence, notwithstanding the price of hire is paid, not only the public, but that individual labourer is injured, by being deprived of that share of the product of his labour which, if the labour had been properly directed, would have flowed from it. Hence the delusion is evident. It will, moreover, be afterwards proved that he does not receive sufficient for his hire.

But it will be found that the principal cause which draws off the labour from the cultivation of the land, is the last mentioned; viz. compulsion.

By the unequal distribution of wealth in most civilized states, the people are divided into the two orders before mentioned; namely, the rich and the poor. In the hands of the former, are lodged those things of every kind which compose what is generally called wealth. In one class of the rich all the lands are vested;

in another, the cattle and the corn raised on them; in a third, the raw materials, tools, machinery, &c.; in a fourth, the goods now manufactured and stored for sale; and so on. In those, or some other class of the rich, all those things are collected, and by the laws firmly secured to them, which the poor man stands in need of, and are necessary to the support of his existence. The persons in the possession of these things hold them out to the poor labourer, saying "If you will labour for me in such and such a way, I will give you out of those things such as you stand in need of; but unless you will do those things which I require of you, you shall have none of them." Hence there is an absolute necessity, under the penalty, the heaviest of all penalties, namely the deprivation of such things as are necessary to his and his family's existence, for his submitting to do the things thus imposed on him to do.

And as the quantity of the necessaries of life, that are or can be consumed by the rich, are limited, and in the purchasing of which a small part only of their wealth can be expended, the surplus they are naturally inclined to lay out in procuring the conveniences, the elegancies, and luxuries of life; these are the produce of the more refined manufactures of different kinds; and for these they are inclined to give a greater price, considering their wealth would be of little use to them if it only procured the common necessaries: hence a much greater proportion of their incomes is expended on those articles: of course a greater proportion of the labouring hands are forced to apply their industry in the various fine manufactures, in which only they can get employ. By these means, hands are drawn off powerfully from agriculture and such coarse manufactures as produce the things that they themselves make use of.

From the foregoing statements, it seems, the following conclusions may be drawn.

1st, That the scarcity which lately and frequently has prevailed, was real.

2d, That the general cause of scarcity is, that too small a number of hands is employed in agriculture.

3d, That the cause why so few are so employed is, that too many are thrown into the manufactures.

4th, That the cause why so many are thus forced into the manufactures is the wealth of the rich.

As it appears that it is the wealth of certain individuals that is the cause of the taking off the labourers from agriculture, by which the scarcity of the necessaries of life is occasioned; and of driving them into the manufactures; of course it must be the cause, not only of the scarcity alleged, but also of all the hardships suffered by the manufacturers, and the poor in general: it seems, therefore, to be the cause of the whole evil. This being the case, the nature and effects of wealth ought to be inquired into; which we now proceed to do.

# SECTION IX.

## OF THE NATURE AND EFFECTS OF WEALTH.

Dr. Smith, in his elaborate work on the Nature and Cause of the Wealth of Nations, has no where given any definition of it.

We have before said, that wealth is usually supposed to consist in the possession of such things as mankind by general consent set a value on; as land, cattle, gold, silver, precious stones, &c. But it seems doubtful whether such things can be considered as constituting the essence and nature of wealth; since the possession of them may sometimes be so circumstanced as that they may be of no value to the possessor; thus, for instance, lands in some uninhabited parts of America. Gold, silver, precious stones, and every other article of that kind, may be, on many occasions, and in many places and circumstances, of no value or use to the owner; and they are to be considered as wealth only in such places where they will be taken in exchange for, and command, such things as the possessor stands in need of, or has an inclination for; all which are the produce of the labour of man. The possession, therefore, of those things which can obtain and command the labour of man, is to be considered as wealth. Wealth, therefore, is the possession of that which gives power over, and commands the labour of man: it is, therefore, power; and into that, and that only, ultimately resolvable.*

It is no argument that wealth is not power, because this power is not extended to the disposal of the lives of the poor; since that would be an extension only of the same power, and differing only in degree.

It will be allowed, that the collected number of persons who possess the aggregate quantity of all such things as compose wealth, have the command and direction of the labour of those who are

* It is remarkable that an old poet should say:—Δυνάμις πέφυκε τοις βροτοις τα χρήματα.

not

not possessed of any of them. It is true, that no individual of the poor is obliged to work for any one individual of the rich; but for one or other of them he is obliged to work, under the penalty of their withholding from him the things without which he cannot live. He is not obliged to work for A, B, C, or D, &c.; but for some one or other of them he is under the unavoidable necessity of working, and at that kind of work, too, they please to require of him. And this power of the rich is as strong and effective as that of the most absolute monarch that ever lived, as far as relates to the labour of the poor; indeed probably more so, since it is doubtful whether any power ever existed, in any kind of government whatever, that could impose on the people what is imposed on them by the power of wealth. To condemn so many to the mines; to confine such numbers to such nauseous, irksome, unwholesome, destructive employments; is more than equal to any kingly power on earth. To enforce the execution of such punishments, would require an army

almost

almost equal in number to the people so punished. The punishments of tyrants are generally confined to those that are near them; but the power of wealth pervades the whole country, and subjects every poor man to its dominion.

If we further consider the nature of the power that wealth gives the rich, in most civilized countries, over the poor, in our times, we shall find it very similar to, and that it arises from the same source with that which antiently the great allodial lords, and the feudal barons of almost all Europe, exercised over their vassals. This will appear from the following passage, extracted from Dr. Adam Smith.

" The wealth of the great lords and ba-
" rons (of almost all Europe) consisted
" almost wholly in lands and the stock on
" them ; and at this time, there being no
" commerce, or any of the finer manufac-
" tures, the great proprietor, having no-
" thing for which he could exchange the
" greater part of the produce of his lands,
" which is over and above the mainte-
" nance of the cultivators, consumes the
" whole in rustic hospitality at home. If
" this

" this surplus produces sufficient to main-
" tain a hundred or a thousand men, he
" can make no other use of it than to
" maintain a hundred or a thousand men.
" He is at all times, therefore, surrounded
" with a multitude of retainers and depen-
" dents, who, having no equivalent to give
" in return for their maintenance, but
" being fed entirely by his bounty, must
" obey him.

" The occupiers of land were in every
" respect as dependent on the great pro-
" prietor, as his retainers. Even such as
" were not in the state of villainage, were
" tenants at will, and depended on his
" good pleasure."

These great proprietors of land, having in their possession all the necessaries of life, forced from the people submission and obedience. Hence it is evident, that it was wealth, both in antient and modern times, that was the origin, foundation, and essence of power; or, in other words, constituted power itself.

In the times prior to the introduction of manufactures and commerce, few men being

being employed in them, of course more were left to cultivate the land, and consequently we may suppose the produce was more proportionate to the number of the people; besides that considerable numbers of them shared the hospitality of the lords, abbeys, &c. Hence the poor of those times, besides being exempted from the pernicious employments of the manufactures, enjoyed a much greater plenty of the necessaries of life than in the present times.—Adam Smith thinks Mr. Hume has great merit in having been the first that observed that manufactures had abolished the servile dependence of the people on the great feudal barons; but Dr. Smith was not aware of this new species of dependence of the lower orders on the rich, which is established in its stead, in most civilized states.

Wealth, or rather the unequal distribution of it, having been shown to be attended with such effects, it is necessary to inquire shortly into its origin, as well as the justice and expediency of it.

Montesquieu considers the system of property,

property, of most of the nations of Europe, as originating in the woods and pastures of Germany. Whilst these tribes of herdsmen and shepherds remained in their own country, certain lands were annexed to each tribe, proportionable to it, and held in common by the whole tribe, and not possessed by individuals in severalty. Afterwards, when they invaded the neighbouring nations, as Italy, Francc, Britain, in order to insure their conquests, and keep the conquered in subjection, it was thought necessary to make a division of the lands they had now got possession of. In what manner and on what principles this was done, Dr. Robertson thinks cannot now be determined with any certainty. There is no nation of Europe, he asserts, whose records reach back to this remote period, and that there is little information to be got from the uninstructive and meagre chronicles compiled by writers ignorant of the true end, and unacquainted with the proper objects of history. But Dr. Gilbert Stewart, in his View of Society in Europe, appears to have taken more pains in making inquiries into these remote trans-

transactions*. The king or leader of the horde, according to him, upon their obtaining possession of any one of the Roman provinces, (which all Europe consisted of at that time) as being of the highest dignity, had the most considerable portion; which constituted his domain. Every warrior, in proportion to his rank, had his lot or share, which gave rise to allodiality. That part of the territory which was not parted out to individuals, was considered, agreeably to their antient ideas, as belonging to the community, and was called the lands of the fisch.

The sovereign took the subsequent division of these, annexing to all of them the burden of presenting themselves in arms at his call. Hence possession flowed to the chiefs, under the burden of presenting themselves in arms at the call of the sovereign. The chiefs dealt out lands to their retainers, under the like injunction, of continuing to them their aid†.

* We must refer to the authorities produced by him.

† This distribution of the land was intended as a military arrangement, in order to keep the people in subjection, which effect it equally has at present,

In this manner, the whole land was parcelled out among the first invaders, and those who soon after followed them; together with the stock on it; for it is not to be supposed that those people who seized the land would abstain from taking the stock on it. As the land, and the stock on it, composed at this time almost the whole of property or wealth, the bulk of the people were, by the above division, bereft of all property. The number of the invaders cannot be ascertained, but, whatever it might be, it would bear a small proportion to the natives; hence a state of unequal property, in as great a degree as at present, was at once established, and is the basis of the present system of property in most of the states of Europe. The change made afterwards by certain conquerors respected only some individuals of their followers, providing for some of them out of the lands that were not distributed, or taking them from the former great proprietors and bestowing them on certain persons who contributed to their conquests.

Whether any political measure that was

unjust at the time of its institution, can become just by time, is a question that ought to be solved. It seems to me, that time can have no effect in changing the nature of it, with respect to its justice or injustice; except it has an effect in altering the evil that first attended it; that is to say, except time removes the hardships and sufferings which the measure brought on the people at its first institution, it can have no effect in removing the charge of injustice imputable to it. If these remain, the same injustice attends the continuance of it that attended the first institution of it.

In such places where an invasion, as that of the Germans on the Roman provinces, did not happen, the appropriation of portions of land to individuals took place probably before any historians arose to record it. In what manner, and on what principles this was done, Dr. Robertson, as we have before seen, thinks, cannot now be determined with any certainty. From the earliest accounts that are authentic, we find the land, in large tracts, in the hands of great allodial lords, and other great

great proprietors, throughout great part of Europe. As this happened long before there was any commerce, or any other means by which large estates are sometimes acquired in our times, they must, most probably, have had their rise in a manner somewhat like the following. Long after men were first placed in the world, the land, no doubt, was common to all, as it is at this day to the inhabitants of many parts of the world, North America, Tartary, &c. where the people, notwithstanding, are very far from being barbarous or savage. In this situation of things, some daring spirits arose, and seized certain parts to themselves, and their conduct was imitated by others. This, probably, must be the original foundation of exclusive property in land; for what other can possibly be supposed? The land being in the first instance common, no person could have any exclusive right to any part of it, except we can suppose that there were certain persons who had, by some public service, obtained a grant of it from the public. Nothing of this kind could probably

bably have happened in those early times, at least to many; or, if it had to some few, could such grant be valid any longer than for the lives of the granters? for they could have no natural right to grant it away from the next generation; every succeeding generation having an equal right, to the use of the land, with the preceding. No person, therefore, could originally have an exclusive right to any portion of land, except perhaps to such a quantity of it as was sufficient to furnish himself and family with the necessaries of life; for, to that quotum of the *produce* he had a right in its common state. This argument is so evident as to require no proof, except to people who, having imbibed the idea of exclusive property in land in their infancy, have suffered it to remain in their minds unexamined the rest of their lives; or to such other people whose interest blinds them so as not to see the clearest truths. Arguments, therefore, to convince the understanding, are probably useless: if any can have effect, it must be such as tend to induce people

people to prefer justice to their interest*.

I shall, however, say somewhat further on the subject.

But whether the assumption of lands and other property, as it is called, naturally belonging to the whole people, into the hands of a few, can be supported on the principles of justice and reason, or not; they may, it has been said, on those of expediency or utility. Thus it has been alleged, that if property were not to be acquired, and held out as a reward of labour and industry, mankind would be indolent and inactive, having no stimulus to exertion.

In my apprehension this is directly contrary to what really happens. Things of every kind being already appropriated and in the possession of certain persons, and firmly secured to them by the laws;

* If the principle of exclusive and perpetual property in land be just, the person that possesses it, having an absolute dominion over it, may direct it to lie barren; and if one possessor has a right do so, all have: and thus they have a right to destroy the rest of mankind. But this consequence being absurd, the premises must be false.

the prizes, which might be held out to be gained by the many, are taken, as it were, out of the wheel; and the chance of a man, without education or connexion, (which is the condition of the great mass of mankind) of bettering his fortune by any efforts of his own, is a thousand to one against him; so as utterly to act as a discouragement to all attempts of that kind. Whereas, had every man his portion of land, his wants and his necessities would naturally induce him diligently to cultivate that which he sees would infallibly supply them *.

But if property or wealth is power, if

* "Property is founded on the good of society; if we abstract from that, it is entirely without foundation." Hume's Essays, vol. ii. note T. page 253.

Does the husbandman, who works for his shilling a day, without having any interest in the produce of his work, and knowing that eight-tenths of it will go to other people; does he, I say, work so cheerfully and industriously as he would do, if he worked on his own land, and would be entitled to the whole produce, the corn, the wine, and the oil, that come from it? In the present system, the people of landed property being few in number, few only receive encouragement to industry on it, from the possession of it. The people of no property being the many, the many receive discouragement, from being deprived of it.

it appears to be, in most civilized states, a power acting over the great mass of the people, to their disadvantage; it will not be easy to show on what principle, either of justice or expediency, it can be defended.

It seems that means ought to be used to prevent any power, of what nature soever it be, from growing up in the hands of one set of subjects to oppress all the rest; and that the joining liberty and property together, as is so frequently done, is to join two things together which are opposite in their natures, and destructive of each other.

"If you should see," says Dr. Paley, "a flock of pigeons in a field of corn; "and if (instead of pecking where and "what it liked, taking just as much as it "wanted and no more), you should see "ninety-nine of them gathering all they "got into an heap, reserving nothing for "themselves but the chaff and refuse; "keeping this heap for one, and that the "weakest perhaps and worst pigeon of "the flock; setting round and looking "on all the winter; whilst this one was "devouring,

" devouring, throwing about, and wasting
" it; and if a pigeon, more hardy and
" hungry than the rest, touched a grain
" of the hoard, all the others instantly
" flying upon it and tearing it to pieces;
" if you should see this, you would see
" nothing more than what is every day
" practised and established among men.
" Among men you see the ninety and
" nine toiling and scraping together an
" heap of superfluities for one; getting
" nothing for themselves all the while,
" but a little of the coarsest of the pro-
" vision which their own labor produces;
" and this one too oftentimes the feeblest
" and worst of the whole set, a child, a
" madman, or a fool; looking quietly on,
" while they see the fruits of their labor
" spent or spoiled; and if any one of
" them take or touch a particle of it, the
" others join against him, and hang him
" for the theft.

" There must be some very important
" advantages, to account for an institu-
" tion which, in the view of it above given,
" is so paradoxical and unnatural.

" Inequality of property, in the degree

"it exists in most countries of Europe, "abstractedly considered, is an evil; but "it is an evil which flows from the rules "concerning the acquisition and disposal "of property, by which men are excited "to industry, and by which the object of "their industry is rendered secure and "valuable."

Vid. Arch. Paley's Philos. of Morals.

Dr. Paley here acknowledges the inequality of property to be an evil: but justifies it,

First, by supposing it to flow from the rules for the acquisition of, &c.

Secondly, by supposing it to encourage industry.

As to the first supposition, that inequality of property did flow from any rules or laws of society, or from the necessary or spontaneous operation of society, we have seen to be contrary to historical facts; it being effected, as appears from them, by arbitrarily and violently dispossessing the original possessors of the land, and distributing it amongst a small, comparatively, number of others, in much larger quantities

quantities than it is at present; and that the consequences of society, or civilization, have been directly of the contrary kind; namely, to lessen much that inequality.

As to the second supposition, viz. that it promotes industry; we have endeavoured to show that it has a contrary effect, and greatly discourages it; by rendering the attainment of property so difficult to the bulk of mankind, as to be nearly impossible, and therefore hopeless.

Dr. Paley adds, "that if there be any "great inequality unconnected with this "origin, it ought to be corrected." From which passage we may infer—that as it implies a doubt whether there be any great inequality, not occasioned by the rules, &c. or not—it ought to be made a subject of inquiry; and further, that Dr. Paley's opinion differs not substantially from Mr. Hume's, viz. that it depends on it's utility.

But if we admit both the suppositions above-mentioned, we still think that inequality

equality of property is injurious to mankind; the effect of it being to bring poverty and misery on the many; whilst it only gives riches to the few, and does not render them happy.

It may be said that wealth might be justly acquired by industry and œconomy.

If wealth is power; if men are born equal and independent of each other; and that * equality and independence are unalienable; if wealth is a power destroying that equality and independence; if it reduces the bulk of mankind under the subjection of the few; all those authors who have defended the inequality of property, not having considered wealth in that light, will by many be considered as having said nothing on the subject. What they have said is of something else, not of wealth; of which they had formed no just idea. They had no idea that the chief acting and effective power in most civilized states was that of wealth; and that most other

* This is true, if by this word an equality of rights only be understood.

powers

powers sprung from, and were supported by it. Neither had they conceived any notion of the effects of it; all arguments, therefore, which they have drawn in its favour, from the utility and expediency of it, even if these were real, are of little weight.

Property, as it is established in most civilized states, may be considered in a light in which it has been seldom seen. The possession of land, cattle, corn, and other things which the land produces, at the same time that it confers a benefit and an advantage on the possessor, occasions a prejudice and a disadvantage to the non-possessor; it is acquisition in the one, it is deprivation in the other. Further, it gives an influence and a power to the person possessing, over the person not possessing. It subjects the non-possessor to an influence and power to be exercised over him by the possessor, and the consequences of it are highly injurious to him. Wealth is an advantage to the possessor only, as it is a disadvantage to the non-possessor; and exactly in the same proportion. If it gave

gave no claim on, no power over, brought no disadvantage to the non-possessor, it would give no claim to, no power to, no advantage to the possessor. What the possessor has, the non-possessor is deprived of.

The situation of the rich and the poor, like the algebraic terms *plus* and *minus*, are in direct opposition to, and destructive of each other. The original acquisition or assumption of land, therefore, to be just, required merit in the person on whom it was bestowed, or by whom it was assumed, equal to the value of it; and a demerit in the person, or the public, from whom it was taken, by which they had forfeited their right to it. To prove the two cases, the one positive, the other negative, is incumbent on those that pretend to support the justice of the original foundation of the exclusive property in land. But how can this be done? What action or service could the original great proprietor of land do the people, by which he could deserve a large proportion of the land of the nation, and a great part of the labour

labour of the people, appending to it? On the other hand, what crimes could the whole of the people commit, that they should have forfeited their right to it? or if they could, how could their posterity be affected by it?

Whatever things a man makes with his own hands, out of such materials as his proportionate share of land yields, must be allowed to be his own; and these may be accumulated, if they are not consumed by the maker of them; or they may be exchanged for other things, made by and belonging to other people, of an equal value; to be strictly estimated by the quantity of the labour employed in making the things exchanged. These things, so made or obtained by fair exchange, and accumulated, may be given to children or others.

The goods, chattels, or personal effects as they are called, acquired in this manner, cannot easily be heaped up to any great degree. The person that succeeds to the chattels, made and saved by the first person, can only add to them what his own

hand

hand makes, and, not being consumed by himself, accumulates. And as this industrious turn never happens to be the disposition of several succeeding generations, the accumulation can never be considerable.

But if we should even suppose that the chattels made in several generations were accumulated in the hands of certain persons, they would be attended with no great inconvenience. The goods would remain a harmless heap; giving no power to the possessor; by which only wealth is hurtful: because, if every person had an allotment of land, the labour of the people would remain free and under their own direction, and the necessaries of life would be attainable by every one; and of course none of the evil of the present state of property, which exists in most civilized nations, would be experienced.

Fortunes may be acquired in a kind of intermediate way, that is, by a method between that by which wealth is raised, by assuming land in the manner as before represented; and that by which a fortune

is

is made by accumulating only such things as are the work of a man's own hand. This third or intermediate method is by trade.

Trade or traffic consists in buying and sleling articles already produced by the poor, and gaining a profit on them. These articles are all the product of the hands of the labourers, manufacturers, &c. from whom they are obtained for less than their full value : a profit otherwise could not be made on them. The tradesman, therefore, shares or takes part of the fruits of the labour of the poor. The justice of this mode of acquiring wealth is by no means so clear as of the latter of the two above mentioned.

The means enabling tradesmen to share a part of the product of the labour of the poor, is their capital, which puts it in their power to furnish materials to the artificers to work on, and to provide them with immediate subsistence ; and on that account is supposed to give the tradesmen a just claim to a part of the productions of the workmen's hands. It becomes neces-

sary,

sary, therefore, to inquire into the nature of this capital.

The capitals of tradesmen consist of stores of such articles as they get up by means of the labour of artificers that work under them. They may have other wealth, but that is not the subject of the present disquisition. From those stores of goods they can supply the people that are in want of them. A very great proportion of such people are the owners of land, and the occupiers of it; those, to wit, that have in their possession the necessaries of life: the tradesmen or manufacturers, therefore, having such things as the possessors of the necessaries of life stand in need of, or have a desire for, and are supplied with, have a claim on these necessaries of life, and may be considered as possessed of a certain share of the land, and the produce of it. They have a claim on it resembling that of a mortgagee, who has a property in land equal to the interest of the sum he advances on it; that is, he has a claim on a part of the productions of it to that annual amount. Now, therefore,

fore, this capitalist, this manufacturer, is in reality a possessor of land, and, like him, has in his power and disposal a certain quantity of the necessaries of life, and can grant or withhold these in the same manner as his joint proprietors, as they may be called, may do*. The manufacturer therefore forces his workmen to work for him, and to give him a share of what the work produces, in the same manner as we have shown the other proprietors of land or possessors of the necessaries of life do; for, the poor are under a necessity of working for him on the terms held out, or go without the things on which they subsist. They have no alternative but to work for him, or for another from whom they can have no other terms. There is no voluntary compact equally advantageous on both sides, but an absolute compulsion on the part of masters, and an

* Or the manufacturer and tradesman may be considered in the view of the land proprietor, only as agents, or *locum tenentes*, to whom they delegate a part of their authority; that is, they make over to them, as it were, a part of the necessaries of life, which their estates produce; the disposal of which gives them the command over the labour of the poor.

absolute

absolute necessity on the part of the workman to accept of it; and which, therefore, might be considered just as the taking so much from the workman by the master: and, of course, fortunes amassed in this manner cannot be just.

It is easily seen that the acquisition of fortunes by tradesmen is in reality nothing but a participation of landed property, which is the basis, the source, and substance of all wealth, and into it all must be resolved.

---

## SECTION X.

### THAT WEALTH IS THE CAUSE OF ALMOST ALL POWER, IN MOST CIVILIZED STATES.

In a preceding chapter, we have endeavoured to show that wealth is power over the labour of the poor. But it seems that wealth is not only a certain definite species of power in the rich over the labour of the poor; but that it is a great means of procuring

procuring for, and securing to the possessors of it, the power of almost every kind which exists in the generality of civilized states. The wealthy part of these states have in their hands all power; the legislative, the executive, and judiciary, in all their branches, viz. ecclesiastical, magisterial, martial, &c. The poor man having a vote in certain cases, gives no introduction to any of these; the vote of a poor man being almost always directed by some kind of influence or other of the rich. And if that was not the case, the representatives or delegates chosen are generally of the order opposite to that of the poor. The rich, therefore, of such states form an aristocracy, in which the effective power is lodged: for, although the forms of government established in different nations may be various, they are generally so in appearance only, not in effect. These forms of government are either monarchical or republican. As to the first of them, i. e. absolute monarchy: in no single man, at least in no hereditary succession of single men, could the authority be supported by any means personal or inherent in himself.

self. He is supported by those who have power, whom we have shown to be the rich, and who have an especial interest to support him in his situation: for all those, by supporting his authority, expect in return that the same authority shall be employed to preserve to them those things from which they derive the power to support him. It is not the person that holds such authority and employs the power, but the persons that gave and uphold the power in him, that are the real rulers of the land: these are the wealthy, i. e. the aristocracy, in almost every civilized country.

In the republican government this is more obvious; since, in these times, it is wealth universally that puts power into the hands of those that have it.

I have often imagined that the first state of things might be aptly represented by a cylinder of a great length, but whose thickness or base was too small for it, when placed perpendicularly, to continue in that position. Around this towering royal cylinder, other cylinders, about two-thirds of its height, are placed; these may represent

represent the late princes of the blood in *France*: to these another row is put, somewhat shorter, composed, as we may say, of dukes, archbishops, &c.: next follows a circle of cylinders, which we call counts, barons, bishops: after this another, of knights, and other men of great landed estates: then a row of cylinders representing merchants, master manufacturers, wholesale dealers: lastly, one of lesser land-holders, &c. &c.; each succeeding row lessening in height. The individuals of each row standing close to each other, and every inferior one closely encircling the next above it, the whole body becomes compact; and having now acquired a broad basis, it stands firm and immovable against the utmost efforts of all the rest of the people, how superior soever they may be in numbers. This conical figure would equally resemble a republic, if the first cylinder was a little shortened.

## SECTION XI.

### ON MANUFACTURES, TRADE, AND COMMERCE.

The rich having obtained the means of commanding the labour of the people, as it seems, had in the next place to direct it so as to enable themselves to enjoy as much of the fruits of it as was possible. We have seen that, under the first great proprietors, in most civilized countries, almost the whole of the people were employed in agriculture, a few only in the coarser trades excepted; of the produce of these, the great lords themselves could use but a small part. What was over and above the maintenance of the cultivators, was given to retainers and followers. Instead, therefore, of continuing to dispose of the produce of the land in that manner, they induced ingenious men to employ their time in the production of works of art, of various kinds, in greater number, variety, and neatness of execution, than heretofore;

heretofore; and rewarded these artisans liberally with what they had been accustomed to give their retainers; and probably with some part of that which they before allowed those, who worked on the land, to keep for their own use.

In this manner, manufactures were introduced; and, by their means, the rich man can now find something for which he can exchange the whole surplus produce of his estates; and thus enjoy and consume himself the whole value of them; sharing little or nothing of them with other people.

The manufactures soon became the employment of a great proportion of the people, and made a very great alteration in the situation of them: and as this forms a very striking feature in the face of civilized countries, and is of great consequence, we think it deserves particular notice and discussion.

In the different ages of the world, statesmen have had different notions with regard to what was most for the interest and advantage of the people. The Romans thought they could not by any means so effectually

effectually promote the welfare of the republic as by conquest. In more modern times the planting of colonies has been adopted with the same view. At present, trade, manufactures and commerce, are the great and enviable objects of European and rival states. The two former methods, having been found not to answer the expectations entertained of them, have been in a great measure given up. Whether the latter is productive of more really good effects, is now to be examined.

Manufactures are the different articles worked up of the raw materials the land produces, as wool, cotton, metals, glass, hides, and are the subjects, or articles as they are called, of trade and commerce; of which the former is carried on within the dominions of a state, the latter with some other nation or people.

Trade and commerce consist in the exchange of one commodity for another, either by the intervention of money, or immediately by barter. In both cases it is really the interchanging one commodity for another. For, though a people dispose of their goods at home or abroad, without receiving

receiving any thing but money, the same money is again laid out in some article which they find is wanted ; they therefore do receive, though not immediately, other articles in exchange for their articles. It is therefore, in effect, barter.

Now, as trade consists in the exchange of one article for another, the advantage or disadvantage of it must depend on this simple circumstance, namely, whether the thing received is more useful and beneficial, to the receiver, than the article parted with. This is the criterion of a good bargain in private concerns, and must be the same in all other kinds of dealings. Hence any trade, whether foreign or domestic, however boasted of, is injurious to the parties or nations concerned, if the things received are not really more useful than the things disposed of.

To examine and try every article that is received and disposed of in large trading nations, by this touchstone, would occasion much trouble. We must be contented therefore to bring to the trial some few of the prime ones.

Those articles are to be considered as

prime,

prime, which are first in degree of necessity; such as corn, flesh-meat, coarse clothing and bedding, warm and dry houses, &c. These are of indispensable and general use.

When the advantages or disadvantages of trade have been treated of, it has been usual for most states to consider any branch of it as advantageous or not, according as the balance is in their favour or against them: if it is in their favour, without any further inquiry it is pronounced to be beneficial. With regard to the money received for the balance, I would ask of what use it is, if not to enable them to purchase some other article of which they stand in need, or are desirous of; and to what other use do they put it? It would therefore have been precisely the same thing if they had received a greater number of articles, provided they had suited their purpose, so as to have made the accounts even in the first instance. But this is a matter not much connected with my subject.

All articles that are exported may be looked upon as of prime use; for whatever these articles might be, however refined and

and unnecessary, yet the labour that produced them, if otherwise directed, would produce those articles that are of prime use and necessity. Hence, whatever manufactures any states export, however superfluous to them, they are to be considered in an opposite light. We have therefore no occasion to examine the nature of the things which are exported.

But with respect to the articles imported, the case is otherwise; they must be all examined by the rule laid down; though it is, in this place, only possible to examine a very small number of them.

The chief parts of the world from whence are procured the great importations to Europe, are the East and West Indies, Spanish America, Turkey, &c. &c. From these places are drawn, tea, silks, muslins, china, gold, rum, sugar, &c. &c. The other articles imported from all these and other places, are, in general, like those specified, such as administer to refinement in dress, equipage, furniture, buildings, the table, &c. Indeed, from those distant places, it would not answer the merchant's views to bring the gross and bulky articles,

such

such as are those of prime necessity *. Of these imported goods, therefore, very few indeed come down to the use of the poor. Hence, therefore, it is evident, without any further enumeration, that the effect of trade and commerce, with respect to most civilized states, is to send out of their countries what the poor, that is, the great mass of mankind, have occasion for; and to bring back, in return, what is consumed almost wholly by a small part of those nations, viz. *the rich.* Hence it appears, that the greater part of manufactures, trade, and commerce, is highly injurious to the poor, as being the chief means of depriving them of the necessaries of life, and is the principal cause of all their calamities.

This is far different from the common notion of the effects of trade: people, somehow or other, imagine that trade has some unknown beneficial effects; that giving employment, and furnishing the

* The articles of commerce, being chiefly the refined manufactures, require much greater labour than is employed in producing the necessaries of life; hence, large quantities of the latter are sent away to procure a small quantity of the former.

necessaries

necessaries of life, are the same thing: but this cannot be the case, except the labour, as has been said before, is actually directed to produce them; which can only be done by agriculture, and the coarser manufactures; or when such things as their labour does produce, are exchanged for the necessaries. To conceive that trade can operate in any other way, is somewhat like reviving the old exploded notions of occult qualities.

The refined manufactures are all produced by long continued labour; the labour increasing according to the fineness of the article. A point-lace veil, worn by the ladies, is perhaps the work of many years of the lace-maker: in the same manner, all the exquisitely finished articles of dress, equipage, the table, furniture, &c. are the productions of long time and tedious application. The rich, by the use of these, consume, in a short time, the work of many people, continued for many days, months, and years: and this is the principal effect of refined manufactures, the enabling the rich to consume the produce of great labour in a short time; or, in other words, to commit greater waste than it would otherwise be in their power to do. We have heard of great men's cooks boiling down several hams, several legs of beef, many joints of veal, fowls, &c. to make a pint or two of soup; which, after all, makes but a small part of the dinner of their masters. The art of the fine manufacturer and that of the cook have precisely the same effect, viz. the bringing together and reducing the bulky matters to their quintessences, as it were; by which means, the great man can consume and destroy, in a very short time, the works of months and of years.

And this effect of enabling the masters of mankind to do more mischief than they otherwise could do, constitutes the great utility of the fine arts, as they are called.

Hæ tibi sunt artes.——VIRG.

Manufactures, besides occasioning that great waste of the labour of the poor, which we have ascribed to them, have a still further bad effect, namely, that they furnish the most certain, if not the only means of oppressing and enslaving a people.

ple. It would be difficult, perhaps impossible, for any species of government, whether a monarchy or an aristocracy, to oppress them greatly and generally, by any other method than by the introduction of manufactures.

There are but two ways of oppressing a people; the one by taking away their property from them; the other by personal injuries. The former of these may be effected in two manners; either by taking from them the necessaries and conveniences of life, when produced by their labours; or by preventing them from employing their time and labour, in producing the necessaries and conveniences for themselves, and forcing them to labour in the production of such articles as they themselves do not enjoy, but which are made use of by the rich. It is by the refined manufactures that this is done. The common necessaries and coarser kinds of manufactures, that could possibly be used by the rich, would require but little labour of the poor. The rich, if there were no refined manufactures, would have but little inducement to call off any great proportion

portion of the labour of the poor from its being applied to the production of such things as they stood in need of; and to do it without an inducement, through a mere arbitrary spirit, would be, probably, done but by few. It is therefore the produce of the refined manufactures, that tempts mankind to oppress; and is almost the only source from whence oppression comes.

It was in this view the Czar Peter considered manufactures, and for that reason so earnestly endeavoured to introduce them into his own country. If he had nothing to sell, he had nothing to buy the fine things with, that he saw in the European states he visited. He could not send out, from his wide continent, any great quantities of the natural productions of the land, or of the common necessaries of life; and consequently could not much distress his people.

With respect to corporal punishments. In the most tyrannical governments, of any kind, cruel personal treatment seldom descends down to the mass of the people; the objects of it are chiefly among those who

who surround the tyrant, or are placed near the seat of such governments; and it is they only that feel the effects of wanton cruelties; such as are inflicted with no other inducement, than the pleasure taken in inflicting them.

If there were no manufactures in India, it would be impossible for the European nations to injure the natives to any great degree. They would only take from them a few of their natural productions, such as cinnamon, pepper, tea, &c. But by means of their manufactures, they can take from them, in large quantities, the necessaries of life, which the labour that produced these manufactures would raise. The natives of India have been deprived of millions, and thousands of millions of bushels of rice, and other necessaries of life, none of which Europeans have received—Europeans have been deprived of millions, and thousands of millions of bushels of wheat, and other necessaries of life, of which the Indians have not received one grain. What Europeans have had from them, or rather what some few of the inhabitants of Europe have had from India,

India, is some fine muslin, China ware, some pearls, some diamonds. What the Indians, or some few of them, have received from Europe, has been some silver, jewelry, clock-work, guilt, carriages, &c. The bulk of the people, on both sides, have been most miserably despoiled by this system of trade, the most pernicious and destructive to the human race, that ever was invented.

## SECTION XII.

### WHY MANUFACTURES AND COMMERCE HAVE BEEN ENCOURAGED BY STATES.

SINCE trade has such mischievous tendency, how comes it to pass that it is so generally encouraged by statesmen, in most civilized nations, and considered in the advantageous light it is?

First, I apprehend it is because some statesmen may not be aware of such tendency.

Secondly,

Secondly, because most manufactured goods of great value may be brought into a small compass, and therefore can be collected and sent any where to market; and, being converted into money, the collection of taxes and other impositions of all kinds is facilitated, which must otherwise be paid in kind; for, though money be the immediate instrument of payment, they are paid, in fact, in manufactures. If, in the first instance, money is made use of when paid out to the creditors of a state, such as an army, navy, pensioners, &c. the same money is by them laid out in manufactures of different kinds, which are consumed by them; money being in this, as in all other cases, like paper or parchment, a mere instrument, to convey property from one to another. In the same manner, in foreign wars, that is, those in which the seat of war is distant from one of the powers engaged, the remittances that are sent abroad are ultimately discharged by goods previously delivered to foreign merchants, or afterwards sent to them; by which such drafts are liquidated. Moreover, the more manufacturers there are

are employed in refined goods, which they do not consume themselves, the greater overplus it gives ministers a feeling in: 1st, by affording more taxable articles;—2dly, because the more manufacturers there are, the greater quantities of goods, as few of them are consumed by themselves, are accumulated; the greater quantity of goods there must consequently be that go to enrich individuals; and the greater the number of rich individuals there is, the greater the number of supporters of their respective governments there will be, in most civilized states; by which governments, in return, the riches and power of these their supporters are secured to them.

---

## SECTION XIII.

### THE INCREASE OF WEALTH AND POWER OF THE FEW, AND POVERTY OF THE MANY.

It is a fact that escapes nobody's observation, that the nature of wealth is to increase in the hands of the possessors. The

The opportunities that wealth gives to acquire more wealth, are very great and obvious. Money gets money, is an old proverb.

That wealth in fact has increased, and is increasing, we have pretty certain indications, in most civilized nations.

First, the great rise in the rent of land is a great increase of wealth, to the possessors of it; and, as will be seen presently, has all the effects of an augmentation of wealth.

Secondly, the great increase of the debt of a nation, is an increase of wealth, however it may appear that an increase of debt should be called an increase of wealth: but this is in fact the character and nature of wealth in all cases, viz. a claim in one person, and an obligation on another. Further, we are to consider that there have been found persons, in some states, who, by the fortunes they have made in trade, and by commerce or otherwise, have been able to advance the prodigious sum of many hundred millions, still keeping their capitals in business, or in land, entire or increasing.

Thirdly,

Thirdly, there is every reason to think that capitals in almost all sorts of businesses are, in most civilized states, increasing. Every appearance seems to countenance such an opinion*. Shops, warehouses, machinery, factories, wharfs, shipping, docks, navigable canals; exports and imports; places of diversion, luxury, and general expensiveness in living, &c. all much increased, in almost all countries.

But what is this increase of wealth; what does it consist of; how is it produced; and what are the effects of it?

Increased wealth may consist of enlarged stores of all those things that are used by man in civilized life; and also in the increase and improvement of all tools, machines, &c. that are used in the making and getting up such things. It may further, as we shall hereafter demonstrate, consist in certain species of incorporeal property, as the claims on a people for the interest of the debt of a nation, i.e. public funds. All these things are wealth to those that possess them, because they give a claim on the labour of the people, and

* See Note O

force from them such things as their labour produces. It is at the same time an increase of poverty in the people, as it subjects them to new and additional demands for the produce of their labour. The people, in order to satisfy these further claims, are obliged to employ more of their time in furnishing those things thus claimed of them; and of course still less of their time and labour is employed in furnishing such things as they themselves stand in need of—the quantity of these last mentioned things every day decreasing, and consequently the poor becoming every day poorer and poorer, in most states*. Hence the wealth or power of the one increasing, is the cause of the increase of poverty and subjection of the other.

This would be found equally true if considered in the abstract; since it is impossible that a claim in one person over another can subsist, without an obligation

* An additional argument that the poverty of the people daily increases is, that potatoes become every day a greater part of the food of the poor, instead of the much superior farinaceous substances.

in

in that other person to answer that claim.

This increase of wealth or power on the one hand, and poverty and subjection on the other, is brought about not only by those, already in a state of subjection, being placed in a state of still greater subjection; but also because more people are reduced to that state: and this is done by throwing down those people that were a little above the line that divides the rich from the poor, to the other side, or below it: and those also that were poor before are rendered still poorer. And this again is accounted for in this manner: if more men become rich, or those that were rich before become richer, the number of unproductive consumers is increased; and many of those that were before consumers, become by these means greater consumers. Hence, consumption is by both means increased, and, consequently, poverty.

With the increasing wealth, or power of claiming more and more of the labour of the poor, the ability, or faculty as I may call it, of the rich to consume, also increases

creases and keeps pace with it. This happens by their requiring not only a greater quantity of the fine manufactures than before; but by their requiring also that the quantity which they have been accustomed to use, should be wrought with a greater degree of refinement; and this to an indefinite degree; and consequently demanding also an unlimited increase of labour.

Hence there are no bounds to the quantity of labour that the rich may have a power of claiming from the people; and, by consequence, of the diminution of the necessaries of life that remain to the poor for their own use. Hence we have not the comfort to find that the miseries of the poor are arrived at their ακμη, or become stationary; for they are evidently in a progressive state of increase, and that in a great ratio*

That this continual increase of wealth

* And this is the true solution of a problem, so often the subject of inquiry—the rapid and great increase of the expenses in the maintenance of the poor of most countries. And again this fact, viz the increase of those expenses, is a confirmation of my hypothesis; namely, the gradual increase of wealth of the few, and the poverty of the many.

and

and power, has no bounds, seems to be confirmed in the instance of China, where trade, manufactures, and civilization, have been a much longer time established than in any country of Europe; all the effects and consequences of them are of course proportionably increased; so that the miseries of the poor are almost beyond conception. "All accounts of travellers agree, "however inconsistent in many other "respects, as to the low wages of labour, "and in the difficulty which a labourer "finds in bringing up a family, in China. "If by digging the ground a whole day, "he can get a small quantity of rice in the "evening, he is contented. The condi-"tion of artificers is, if possible, still worse. "Instead of waiting indolently in their "workhouses for the calls of their custo-"mers, as in Europe, they are continu-"ally running about the streets, with the "tools of their respective trades, offering "their service, and, as it were, begging em-"ployment. The poverty of the lower ranks "of people in China far surpasses that "of the most beggarly nations in Europe. "In the neighbourhood of Canton,

"many

"many hundred, it is commonly said "many thousand families have no habitation on land, but live constantly in little "fishing-boats, upon rivers and canals. "The subsistence which they find there is "so scanty, that they are eager to lick up "the nastiest garbage thrown overboard "by any European ship. Any carrion, "the carcass of a dead dog or cat, for example, though half putrid and stinking, "is as welcome to them as the most "wholesome food to people of other countries. Marriage is encouraged in China, "not by the profitableness of children, but "by the liberty of destroying them. In all "great towns several are every night exposed in the streets, or drowned like "puppies in the water. The performance "of this horrid office is even said to be "the avowed business by which some "people earn their subsistence." Adam Smith, vol. i. p. 108*.

As the condition of the poor grows

* Adam Smith little thought this increase of poverty was the consequence of the increase of wealth, which he has so laboured to effect.

worse, and their hardships and sufferings become more difficult to be borne, the spirit of resistence will, it is to be feared, show itself in endeavours to throw off their restraints and pressure; first by a greater frequency of thefts of all kinds, house-breaking, highway robberies, &c.; and afterwards by open insurrections. Hence coercive measures will increase, the laws securing property will be multiplied and rendered more severe; a large military force must be kept up; and, in short, a military government established; and to induce the soldiers to act against their fathers and mothers, brothers and sisters, and to forget every natural and moral tie, it will be necessary largely to increase their pay; and in order to alienate and estrange them from their kindred and acquaintance, they must be kept separate from the other subjects, in barracks, garrisons, &c. And then will not this same military body, thus feeling no other sentiment in their breast, with respect to the rest of mankind, than the sense of the power over them which they see themselves

selves in the possession of, soon be the masters of the rich as well as the poor?

---

## SECTION XIV.

### WHETHER THE RICH ARE USEFUL TO THE POOR.

It has been thought, and it was asserted by a man of eminence, a few winters since, that the rich are as useful to the poor, as the poor to the rich. This is a position, I think, that it will be difficult to support. In order to bring it to the test, let us see what each does for the other.

The poor man produces by his labour almost every thing that the rich man eats, drinks, and wears; the house in which he lives; in short, nearly every thing he has or enjoys; for the land would produce few things without the labour of man.

Now, what does the rich man produce for the use of the poor man? Precisely none

none of all the things mentioned. But he gives him money to buy these things with, it is said. In answer to this; it is to be observed, that money only transfers the property of things, which were before produced, from one to another; and what it brings to one it takes from another. The money makes nothing; therefore adds nothing to the mass of the necessaries of life, or other things: it therefore can give to one only what it takes from another. The number of people extended over the world, and the quantity of provisions being also equally extended; we do not see from whom or from whence we take what we give to another, or the parts of which, what we give to another, is composed. But our reason tells us, that if we with our money buy bread to give to a poor man, without adding to the mass of corn; we only give to him what another would otherwise have had, and that we deprive the one of as much as we give to the other. This is true, but may not be evident. By contracting the field from this immensity, we shall better perceive the truth.

To

To illustrate this, we will suppose a ship at sea, whose provisions, it was feared, would not hold out till she arrived in port. The crew, therefore, were put on short allowance. Now, suppose a gentleman, a passenger on board, employing one of the men to wait on him, gave him a shilling a day; with which money the sailor sometimes prevailed on some one of his messmates to sell him part of his scanty allowance. In this case, the gentleman's money just took as much from one as it gave to the other; and therefore was of no service. A country may be compared to a ship, which, though larger than the ship, is still circumscribed; and the quantity of provisions are given as much in the one as the other.

If there had been no intervention of money in the case, this matter would have appeared plain. The rich man could then give nothing to the poor man, except he visibly received it from another: for he has no corn, or any thing else, which his own hands produced, for the use of the poor. Money covers and conceals the action, as the case of a watch does the

motions

motions within; by giving the money, he seems to give the corn. Money is therefore an instrument, serving to deceive and delude the people; and to induce the poor wretches to think the rich their benefactors, whether they are or not.

The rich man has truly nothing to give the poor man; the money, as well as the bread that was bought with it, the poor man's hands had before produced. The rich man produces nothing for the use of the poor man, or for himself. The poor man's labour raised the gold and silver from the mines; and his labour also raised the provisions that the gold and silver purchase. Whether the money or the possessor of the money had ever existed, the necessaries of life, which the money purchases, still would have been furnished for the use of the poor man—by the poor man himself; not only in the same but a much greater quantity, if no part of the labour had been employed in procuring the gold and silver, of which the money is made. The rich are employed in the consumption, not in the production of things.

Notwith-

Notwithstanding the rich man produces nothing, he consumes not only as much as the poor man, but frequently ten times, an hundred times, a thousand, or ten thousand times as much, according to the measure of his wealth. But, what can hardly be conceived, there have been people who have supposed that the rich, by the very act of consumption of the necessaries of life, benefit mankind.

In order to discover whether the rich are useful to the poor, let us examine the question, in the instance of a great proprietor of land.

It is to be considered that the necessaries of life are not the spontaneous growth of the earth; but require, for their production, the labour of man to be bestowed on it. The necessaries of life, therefore, are the joint product of the land and the labour. Whether therefore the land be taken away, or the labour required to cultivate it, be taken away, the effect is the same—the non-production of the necessaries of life: and hence every great land-owner may be said, in effect, to annihilate so much land as those people

ple which he draws off from agriculture, if not drawn off, would cultivate. The absolute quantity of land which he in this manner virtually annihilates is thus ascertained: but the relative quantity of the land which he so annihilates, in respect to what he possesses, must be determined by the proportion his rent bears to the whole value of the produce of his land *. If the rent is equal to half the produce of the land, he is to be considered as the annihilator of half the land he possesses: if the rent is equal only to one-third of the produce of the land, he then is to be looked on as annihilating one-third of the land only.

All these people which he draws off are all the while consuming the necessaries of life in a wasteful manner, and in a much greater quantity than their just proportion, without contributing to reproduce the

* As a great proprietor of land suffers his land to be cultivated, and as the produce of it is consumed by the people, he is not looked upon, by merely receiving his rent, as a person injurious to the people.

smallest

smallest particle of such things as they have consumed. The number of such people, thus rendered not only useless but pernicious to mankind, may be calculated by considering what on an average the earnings of those servants, labourers, tradesmen and artificers, may be: this may probably be about ten or twelve shillings per week, or *25l.* or *30l.* per annum. To get at the number, therefore, we have only to divide the amount of the rent, suppose *40,000l.* by 25, which quotes 1,600; and that is the number of effective men rendered useless and unproductive: and supposing each of these to have four in family besides himself; multiplying therefore the 1,600 by that number, we have 8,000, which is the number of souls that might have been furnished with the necessaries of life by the labour of those hands which have been converted, by this proprietor of land, from productive and useful, to non-productive and consuming ones; and thereby effecting what is equivalent to the annihilation of as

much

much land as would maintain 8,000 people *.

The same income, whether arising from public funds, trade, profits of a profession, or any other source, if spent in the same manner, has exactly the same effects—except as to that arising from tithes, or lands let on restrictive leases: in both these cases additional disadvantages to the public arise, by their preventing the application of the land to the most productive uses.

The Being who made the earth and all the living creatures on it, so constituted the earth that it produces the things necessary for the subsistence of those creatures: and he so constituted those creatures that their existence should depend on those things which the earth produces. It is evident, therefore, that the Creator intended the land for the use of the creatures he has put on it. Consequently, that no creature ought to be cut off from the pos-

* The number of hands drawn off from agriculture, &c. by a land proprietor, will be in proportion to what he spends, i.e. his rent. Hence the mischievous tendency of the rise of rents.

session of some part or other of the earth, and that in such quantity as to furnish him with the necessaries of life. But this, by the system established in most nations of Europe, the persons in possession of the exclusive property of the land, not only have the power of doing, but in effect do it, and thus, depriving them of a sufficiency of the necessaries of life, destroy great numbers every year.

It is difficult to conceive how the lawyer*, who regards the first principles of right and wrong; or the divine †, who professes to be guided by the will of God; or the philosopher ‡, with whom utility and expediency is the basis of justice; can support a doctrine thus contrary to these clear, natural, rights of man; to these evident demonstrations of the intentions of the author of nature; and to those undeniable proofs of its mischievous effects on the great mass of the people.

If the wealthy, therefore, be the greatest and most wasteful consumers of the necessaries of life, and also the greatest impe-

* Blackstone. † Paley. ‡ Hume.

diments to the production of them; they cannot, it is to be feared, be considered as useful to the poor.

We have seen the great mortality among the poor in most civilized countries; we have demonstrated that this is owing to the want of the necessaries of life; we have shown how this want is produced; and consequently what occasions the great destruction among our fellow creatures. This destruction will appear to be greater than any arising from other causes, if we consider the constant and perpetual operation of it. The proofs of the fact must be admitted; and that the facts are brought up to the sources of them, cannot be denied. Yet, notwithstanding all this, it will make little impression on the minds of men. What then can be the cause of this strange phenomenon in human nature? I apprehend it to be this—Although there may be many great men, who have contributed to the death of many persons in the course of their lives; yet no acts of any one of them have ever been solely the occasion of the death of any one person. No one man, how great soever his consumption might

might be, is the sole cause of the want of necessaries of life to any poor individual. But he may contribute in a certain proportion to it. He may contribute a certain part of a cause that destroys 500,000 people annually: suppose that part to be the 500,000th part of the cause of the death of all those that perish, he then destroys equal to one man: as a certain number of parts of a whole makes a whole, or as a certain number of fractional parts makes an integer. There may be many private men, in Europe, who singly furnish not only the five hundred thousandth part, but even more than the five hundredth part of the cause by which the total number is destroyed, in doing which he destroys equal to one thousand people annually.

---

## SECTION XV.

### ON THE DIFFERENT INTERESTS OF THE RICH AND POOR.

We have seen that in many states almost all power is placed in the hands of the

the rich ; it might seem, therefore, that the interest of both is the same ; and that each order by consulting its own interest would at the same time consult that of the other: but it is to be feared that we shall not find that to be the case.

It is obvious that the interest of the buyer and seller is, in every case, opposite. It is the interest of the buyer to give as little for what he buys as he can get it for. It is the interest of the seller to get as much for what he sells as he can get for it. Every rich man is to be considered as the buyer, every poor man as the seller, of labour. It is for the interest of the rich man to get as much of the work of the poor man and to give him as little for it as he can ; in other words, to get as much of the labour, and to give the labourer as little of the produce of that labour as he can help ; the less of the product of his labour, the labourer himself is suffered to consume, the more is left to his employer to take to himself.

The opposition of interest between the poor and the rich is said to be counteracted and cured by the competition subsisting

sisting between the masters or employers; but we shall see that in fact it is no cure, by the small proportion, as is hereafter demonstrated, of the produce of the labour of the poor, that is allowed them. The employers or masters endeavour to lower it, or that it should not rise. The workmen endeavour to raise it; but, being very unequally matched, for the most part, with little success. It has been taken notice of, that the manufacturers, in their disputes with their masters, are generally worsted. If they strike their work with this view, as what they have beforehand is generally very little, they cannot hold out long, but are, like a garrison short of provisions, obliged to capitulate on the best terms they can get. We need not observe that this, the only method they have of redressing their grievances, is frequently crushed by the military *. There are,

* If the poor manufacturers are not allowed to strike their work, they are debarred the right and advantage that all other people have in their dealings—of refusing to take what is offered to them if they think proper. This, together with their having no means of standing out, through their want of immediate supplies, renders them incapable of making a good bargain with

are, in few states, laws to prevent masters from combining for the purpose of lowering wages.

We have said before, that it is for the interest of the rich to get as much of the labour of the poor, and to give the labourer as little of the produce of the labour as he can help. In this instance the labourer is exactly in the case of a farmer's ox or horse. By the labour of the husbandman, and of the horse or ox, is raised the whole produce of the land; the less part of which, i. e. the less corn or hay, the ox or horse has, the more is reserved for the farmer's or proprietor's use. It is the same with regard to the husbandman, though not in so direct a manner. The less money the husbandman receives, the less corn he can buy and eat, and of course, the more the farmer or proprietor takes to himself*. If there is any differ-

with their masters; and the price of their labour is constantly diminishing, though the nominal or money price is increasing, which is the result of other causes. Vide page 85.

* The farmer is to be considered as the agent for the proprietor, who principally enjoys the fruit of the labour of the poor.

ence,

ence, it is in favour of the ox, for the farmer is by his own interest induced to keep it well; but he has no interest in the matter, with regard to the poor labourer's health, &c. If by his excessive labour, in order to maintain a large family, he wears himself out, the farmer sustains no loss as he does by the death of the ox*. The tendency there is continually to a diminution of the wages, and a deterioration of the condition of the poor, is a matter surely to be regretted; and their case is highly entitled to our compassion.

The objects of these two different interests in most civilized states being, on the one side, every thing that relates to the ease and gratifications of the rich; and

* The poor man, who has a large family, in order to provide a little better for them than he can do by his day work, is inclined to take task work, such as mowing by the acre, threshing by the quarter, &c. At these he works harder, and many more hours in the day, allowing himself little rest. There is scarce any kind of the husbandman's work that does not require almost the full exertion of his strength. His toil is therefore immense, and soon wears him out; his joints become stiff, he is bent with labour, and he arrives prematurely at old age.

on the other to whatever relates to the necessaries of life, and of course to life itself; it is not to be wondered at if the parties should be in earnest, in the support of their different claims*.

This is more true with regard to the rich: the determined resolution with which they maintain their wealth and privileges, is very great. The poor, though more nearly concerned, yet being deprived of the means of resistence, as well as depressed and dispirited by the natural effects of their situation, are not equally active in asserting and reclaiming their rights.

* Adam Smith says, civil government, so far as it is instituted for the security of property, is in reality instituted for the defence of the rich, against the poor. Vide *Wealth of Nations*, vol. iii. page 80.

## SECTION XVI.

### WHAT PART OF THE PRODUCE OF HIS OWN LABOUR IS MADE USE OF BY THE LABOURER.

To form a calculation, with regard to what part of the produce of his own labour or work a labourer or workman makes use of, and enjoys himself, we have but few data to proceed on: we have, however, some that will pretty satisfactorily solve the problem. The things which he consumes must be procured by his income; to it, therefore, they must be proportionable, and be limited by it. The earnings are the labourer's income: we have therefore only to see what proportion this income of the labourers, collected, bears to that of the rest of the people, also collected. We have seen before, that the labourer's wages are about 25*l.* per annum: that the number of the labouring people amounts to about eight-tenths

tenths of the whole: that, supposing their families to consist of five persons each, in a nation consisting of ten millions of souls, there will be 1,600,000 families; this multiplied by 25 makes 40 millions; which is the amount in value of what is consumed by the labouring class of people.

It is not an easy thing to obtain the amount of the income of the rest of the people, viz. the rich. But, with regard to our argument, it is the same thing if we get the amount in value of the whole produce of the labour of the poor; for, having done that, if we deduct from it the amount of what is consumed by the poor, the remainder must consequently be what is consumed by the rich.

To speak with respect to England, in this instance: the rent of all the lands in it, about twenty years ago, was supposed by Adam Smith, and others, to be twenty millions; since that time, we may fairly lay it at one-third more, or thirty millions. He also supposes this rent not to be above one-third of the value of the produce of the land. This produce of the land,

therefore,

therefore, may be estimated at ninety millions. Dr. Grey, in his late treatise on the income tax, makes it one hundred and twelve millions. This sum, then, is the amount in value of that species of the produce of the labour of the poor employed in agriculture. The amount of the exported manufactures according to the statement of Mr. Pitt, was, the last year, about fifty millions; the home consumption of manufactures is supposed to be double, and by most authors treble, the foreign: the total produce, therefore, according to these opinions, of labour, is three hundred and twelve millions. The poor themselves enjoy only forty millions, i. e. about one-eighth part, or the produce of one-eighth part of their time.

If this statement is true, eight-tenths of the people consume only one-eighth of the produce of their labour; hence one day in eight, or one hour in a day, is all the time the poor man is allowed to work for himself, his wife and his children. All the other days, or all the other

hours

hours of the day, he works for other people.

> Sic vos non vobis mellificatis, apes :
> Sic vos non vobis fertis aratra, boves.

The conclusion here given, as to the share which every labouring man enjoys of the produce of his labour, is inferred from premises and data which cannot be suspected; being furnished by people who had no design that such a conclusion should be drawn; and who probably would be sorry to find that such an inference could be made from them. The persons too who have formed the calculations and made the statements, were, from their situation and abilities, the best qualified for the task that could anywhere be found. The fact, therefore, that the poor do enjoy exactly or near the share of the product of their labour which has been shown, must be taken as undoubted: and will not every just man deplore the injustice of it, and every humane man commiserate the case of the sufferers? It is surely an essential part of liberty, to

enjoy

enjoy the full fruits of one's own labour. Whether the negro in the West Indies has a less proportion than the above, I cannot determine; but in other respects he seems to have the advantage of the free but poor man of Europe.

Slaves being the property of their masters, like cattle, it is the interest of the owners to keep them alive; and not only that, but to keep them so that they may be in health and vigour to do their work; and that their marriages may be fruitful; and to take the same care of their offspring, and from the same motives, that farmers do of their calves and lambs. But in most places of Europe the poor man does his work, and he receives his wages; but whether he lives an hour afterwards is a matter of little concern to his employer: the same wages will procure the work to be done by another.

But the poor man has not even this small proportion of his labour or time; since Sunday, one day in the week, is taken from him by most churches in Europe, which must be deducted first. He has therefore only a fraction of a fraction,

tion, viz. one-eighth of six-sevenths; that is, about one-ninth.

It might be said, that if the workman receives the wages for his work, that he receives the fruits of his labour: but it is to be considered, that the wages of the labourer are not the fruit or produce of his labour, that is, the things his labour actually makes; but the price the master has agreed to give, and what the workman, in most instances, is compelled to take for or in lieu of the whole produce of his labour: this is sometimes rendered evident, as when the labourer has his wages, as it were, in kind, by receiving a part of the wheat or the potatoes, &c. which his labour has raised: the small part he receives of the whole is then seen.

It may, notwithstanding, seem difficult to be understood, how it happens, that the poor man receives so small a part of the fruits of his own labour, as the one-eighth or the one-ninth, since we know of no master tradesman or manufacturer who has so large a profit on any article made by the poor man.

But

But it is to be remembered, that there are many more people than one, who take a profit on almost every single thing that is turned out by the workman or workmen; for instance, in a coach, there is, first, the master coach-maker, then the master painter, the master colourman; there is the tanner, the currier, the glass plate maker, the draper, the timber merchant, the master smith, the master harness maker, the silver and plate-furniture maker; and under every one of these, there may be a great number of subordinate branches, so that, perhaps, an hundred besides, or many more, draw a profit, and share part in the price the coach sells for, when finished, without doing a stroke of work themselves, at any part of it; insomuch, that the whole price is almost melted down into profit; and probably if the portion that goes to the persons who actually employ manual labour on it, were separated from the whole, less than an eighth would be found to be received by them. These master manufacturers, of different kinds, we number among the rich.

If

If the poor did receive and make use of a greater proportion of the produce of their labour, than is stated to be received by them; how could the rich enjoy and consume so many things, as it is evident they do; and who, it is equally evident, contribute nothing to the production of them? A man of seventy thousand a year consumes equal to the whole produce of two thousand eight hundred workmen, which would maintain as many families; and if these were supposed to consist of five persons each, he consumes the sustenance of fourteen thousand souls. A man of one thousand a year consumes the produce of forty workmen, artificers, &c.; that is, the sustenance of two hundred souls: and so in proportion do men of greater, lesser, and intermediate fortunes, consume. If the consumption of the rich is so great, how can the poor have more to make use of, than what is stated?

The land-owner lets his land to a tenant, who sells part of the produce, which are necessaries of life, to the labourer or workman, for money; which money was previously

viously earned by his labour or work; without which he could not get the money, nor the necessaries of life which the money purchases. It is his work, therefore, that procures the necessaries. Now the work which he does for these, must be what the manufacturer requires of him; and what the manufacturer requires of him, is such things as the land-owner will purchase; i. e. requires of the manufacturer. This land-owner requires, first, a sufficiency of bread and other necessaries of life. Of these he wants but a certain quantity; his income, therefore, which is the annual produce of the necessaries of life from his land; or, which is the same thing, the money which they have been sold for; except what goes for these, goes to purchase costly dress, furniture, equipage, luxuries, &c.; to furnish which, takes up by far the greatest part of the time and labour of the poor.

Now if the labourer himself had land, he would employ a very great part of his time on that land; and the remainder in producing coarse clothing, &c. for himself and his family. All the labour which

he

he now performs, except a small part of that which is bestowed in raising those necessaries of life which he uses himself, is bestowed on other things, of which he enjoys and consumes nothing, but which are consumed by the land-owners, &c. who do nothing: and these amount, as has been before demonstrated, to eight or nine tenths of the whole.

We see in the accounts of travellers in Russia, that most of the nobility there have a great number of their slaves brought up to work at trades and manufactures; and that some of them take a thousand or more to Petersburgh, to remain with them during their winter residence there. Few of the slaves, I suppose, are brought up to the highly refined manufactures; so that their lords are not furnished by them with all such of the most finished ones as they make use of. If they had been so, it would then be seen how many of their slaves were taken up in producing such things as they, the lords, made use of; and how many men were left to raise the necessaries of life; some of which also are used by the lords and their attendants. The proportion we have assigned would then be more evident, but not more certain than it is at present.

The poor cannot eat without money. They cannot get money without labour. Those, therefore, that are in possession of money, or the necessaries of life, have the command of the labour of the poor, by having the power of withholding the necessaries of life from them; and, with regard to the poor, it is entirely the same thing, whether they are compelled to labour for other people, under one kind of penalty or another. The right or power which land-holders have of raising their rents is tantamount to the power of forcing from the poor an unlimited quantity of labour. The common interest of land-owners will always unite them in the measure of raising their rents. But it seems unnecessary to insist longer on such arguments; it is evident to the view. Let any one walk the streets of a great city; let him observe the buildings, public or private, there; the dress, the equipage, &c. of the persons he meets, the multiplicity and the richness of the goods in the shops:

shops: let him from thence go down to the wharfs, quays, &c. and, after having made the tour, let him consider how few of the things he had seen were intended for, or can be obtained by the poor. But all these things are the works of their hands and fingers; and those that appear the most neat, rich, and splendid to the observer, are the productions of the most sordid, nauseous, and destructive employments.

But whether or not in the very complicated state of civilization, occasioned by the intervention of money, and the great division of labour in the manufactures, we could account for, and render visible the manner in which it happens, that the poor workman receives and enjoys so little of the fruits of the labour of his own hands; nothing can be more clearly demonstrated than that he does receive no more of the effects of the sweat of his brow, than what is above represented. If the whole of the productions of the industry of the poor amounts to three hundred millions, and their wages amount only to forty millions, they can purchase only about one-

eighth

eighth or one-ninth of the whole, and of course can enjoy no more.

If every labouring man, who now seems to enjoy only one-eighth or one-ninth of the work of his hands, in most civilized countries, enjoyed the full produce of his labour, he would enjoy eight times as much as he does at present; that is to say, he would enjoy as many of the necessaries and conveniences of life as a person who has an income in those countries of about 150*l.* per annum now does: and if the labour now bestowed on the refined manufactures, was taken off from them, and employed in raising such things as a person of that income usually makes use of, there would be that quantity of them to supply every labourer; that is, every labourer's family in Europe with.

We have, I fear with too much reason, said that, in the present system, about five hundred thousand souls, in communities consisting of ten millions, perish annually, who would probably have lived to mature age, if they had had justice done them, by being suffered to enjoy the fruits of their toil. Probably (for we are not

not furnished with such documents as might enable us to calculate with certainty) the number of people in these communities, who have above the average income of 150*l.* or 200*l.* per annum, is small, not exceeding a few hundred thousands; so that the number of those that contribute at all to the evils complained of, being those whose incomes exceed the above-mentioned sum of 200*l.* per annum, are not very numerous; and those that principally occasion the waste, being people of larger fortunes, are still much less numerous. The question, therefore, is, whether 500,000 souls shall perish annually, and that eight-tenths of all the others should be pinched, distressed, and diseased, in order to furnish this small number with the superfluities.

## SECTION XVII.

### THE STATE OF THE POOR NOT NECESSARILY SUCH AS IT IS.

It has been asserted that the state and condition of the poor, in most civilized countries, is necessarily such as it is; that is to say, it could not be otherwise in the nature of things; considering it as unavoidably flowing from that order and subordination which, say they, must be kept up in every community, and without which, society could not subsist. This is an opinion that the wealthy are very much inclined to entertain and cherish; since it gives them the quiet possession of all their assumed advantages over their fellow creatures.

In the first place, it may be observed that the words* order and subordination,

* This is another instance (the joining the words *liberty* and *property* having been before taken notice of) where two words are joined together, one of which only is admissible; the other, linked with it, having gained admission without having a right to it.

though

though so frequently joined together, have no necessary connexion; if by the word subordination, is understood different degrees of property, as from great wealth to extreme poverty. Order may not only be kept up without such different degrees of poverty as subsists in many civilized states; but with much less difficulty without them, than with them. It would surely be much more difficult to keep men, who were pining with hunger, and starving with cold, in order, and from theft and robbery, than it would men who had no such pressing necessities to urge them to such acts.

Secondly, it appears that the present state of the poor, in most civilized nations, does not flow necessarily, or indeed at all, from the state of civil society; that it is not the effect of civilization, but that, on the contrary, it is the cause of it: it was prior to it; and civilization could not have taken place by any other means than through the previously reduced state of the bulk of mankind. Civilization we have defined to consist in the improvements of the sciences, and in the refinements of manufac-

manufactures, by which the conveniences, elegancies, and luxuries of life are furnished. These things, it is evident, could have had no existence, unless the bulk of mankind had been reduced to be manufacturers; that is to say, till they were reduced to that degree of poverty as to be compelled to work at those trades for their subsistence. The state of the poor therefore does not necessarily follow from civilized society; but the converse of the assertion is true. Let us now, therefore, see from whence it does flow and derive its origin.

We have seen that the Germans, on their first taking possession of the provinces now composing the different states of Europe, took the lands from the natives, and distributed them among themselves; and thus, by one act, wealth on one hand, and poverty on the other, was established, long before the tendency of civil society could be supposed to have given rise to it. Indeed, directly opposite effects have since sprung from civil society, i. e. from refinement in manufactures, &c; for, whatever other effects

effects these have had, the dividing and distributing great masses of land into lesser have been the consequences of it: as is evident from the estates acquired by merchants, manufacturers, &c.

This arbitrary and forcible assumption of land gave rise to, and is the foundation of the inequality of all other species of property, in all or most civilized countries. The great proprietors having it in their power to direct the labour of the poor into what channel they pleased, were inclined to apply it to the production of such things as they themselves would have the exclusive enjoyment of. Of provisions they had as much as they could consume: they directed, therefore, the labour of the poor to the arts. They required the articles in the furniture of their houses to be more numerous, and to be daily increasing in richness, neatness, and elegancy of workmanship: the same happened with respect to their own and attendants' dress, their tables, equipage, &c. To furnish all these things, more men were employed, more became artificers; fewer agriculturists remained.

As

As the articles in these different branches became more refined and complex, it was found that several workmen of different trades were required to finish many single things. Hence, master manufacturers arose, keeping in their employment people who worked at the several branches necessary to get up such complicated pieces of furniture, &c. These articles, as they became more improved, became also more expensive; hence the land-owners were obliged to give more of the produce of their land to purchase them. Many, whose incomes were unequal to their taste for such things, were induced to sell part of their lands to purchase them. Hence the master manufacturers became possessed of landed property. They also gradually became enabled to lay up larger quantities of goods which they had manufactured, thus forming a stock or capital. It now became necessary, in order to dispose of them, to appoint persons whose whole business should be to retail them out: soon after, wholesale dealers were found necessary, merchants, &c. And a great number of another species

of

of rich men were thus raised. At length, things were brought to their present state. And in this manner did the original inequality in the possession of land give rise to the inequality of all property or wealth, and then of course to the low condition of the poor, which therefore was not the consequence of the natural course of society, but was prior to it, and was the effect of the first general seizure of land by the first and other invaders.

But if the tendency of society to produce wealth unequally, were such as asserted, this effect of it, proving detrimental to the bulk of the people, should be counteracted and prevented by such persons as are appointed to see *nequid mali capiat respublica.* If the power of the rich over the poor is an improper power, it ought to be suppressed. The design in the appointment of all government, and of the authority and force put into their hands, is solely to defend the weak against the strong, in whatever manner their strength be obtained or employed to the disadvantage of the people.

This false notion, viz. that the state of the

the poor is necessarily such as it is, has had ill effects. The wealthy, thus considering the matter, have thought themselves under no obligation to relieve the poor, but always imagine what little they do for them to be a work of supererogation, and for which they sufficiently applaud themselves: but if they see that the situation of the poor is occasioned by themselves, is the express act of theirs, and that they are the true cause of all their afflictions, they will then have a different idea of the claim the poor have on them.

But here the great charities of most civilized countries will be brought forward. In the first place, I shall observe that most of the charitable foundations have been made by dying men, when they had neither a right nor a power to retain the lands with which they endowed them. But, without insisting on this, the whole amount of them, when compared to that which is received from the poor, is so small as to deserve no notice: they do not amount to the one-hundredth part of it.

If what the rich gave them was the work of their own hands; if it was what their own labour had produced; if it was what could not have been had without them; there would then, how small soever it was, have been some foundation for their claims to the virtue of charity: but if they only give the poor a part of what the hands of them, the poor, had wrought, of that which had its existence from the poor, and without them would have had no existence; the act seems to me to be of a very different nature.

---

## SECTION XVIII.

### ON THE EFFECTS OF CIVILIZATION ON THE OTHER ORDERS.

We have seen the effects of civilization on the lower classes of mankind; their penury, their diseases and their mortality; their mental faculties almost obliterated; and themselves nearly reduced to machines.

It

If these bad effects were counterbalanced by any good in the other classes, this would somewhat lessen the evil. But it is to be feared that this is not the case. It has ill effects in every order. In the division of the people into two orders, all above poverty have been put into one class. But it is evident that, of those so put together, there must be very different degrees, with respect to wealth. In those of the first degree, the profusion of wealth produces almost the same effects as the opposite extreme, poverty. Those of the middle share probably the fewest evils attending the system. Those of the lowest degree, and many individuals in the other degrees, have constantly before their eyes, and near them, the wretched state of the poor. Hence their dread of it, and their never-ceasing anxiety to preserve themselves and their families from falling into it; into which they see, every hour, some unhappy person or other dropping and overwhelmed.

Hence the epithet, care-crazy, is given the mother by Shakspeare.

In this manner does the system straiten

all

all degrees: with difficulty do they support themselves in the way they have been accustomed to live: a continual struggle and jostling: all endeavour to get up higher, out of the reach of this dreadful gulf,—poverty. Thus rich and poor, all, suffer the ill effects of it—

> Æquè pauperibus nocuum, locupletibus æquè.
>
> HOR.

These things, which are really and necessarily the effect of the system, are ascribed to the unavoidale condition of human affairs, and therefore no remedy is sought for. It is certain, however, that all the evils arise from the cause I have assigned, except that of ill health (and that too is most frequently occasioned by it): and if the cause were removed, the life of man would in general be happy. They arise from the waste and profusion of the opulent, consuming what would be sufficient for the whole people, and also straitening themselves, as well as all other degrees of men.

A small

A small number * of people, in most civilized states, consume the far greater part of the produce of the labour of the whole. Hence, what is left is very short of a sufficiency for the great mass of the people: every man, therefore, seeing that many must go without a sufficient quantity of the necessaries, uses every effort not to be of that number; and is strongly urged to secure what is enough for himself and family. Hence a violent struggle is excited: every man strains every nerve: every man's interest becomes opposite to every man's. Hence eager competitions, sharp contentions, frauds, oppression. Hence the source of all matters that render life anxious and unhappy. This is the cause of all the cares and troubles of life: to this they are solely and wholly to be attributed: to ascribe them to the constitution of human nature, and human affairs, is the artifice of those who have more than their share, and are the cause of the evil. This plainly accounts for the evils; to assign

* Vide Note K.

them to the other cause, is merely gratuitous; is ascribing effects to an occult and undefinable cause, when they may be referred thus clearly and demonstratively to this one simple, evident, and adequate source.

The different ages of the world, the golden and iron ages, are not the fictions of the poets, but are the descriptions delivered down by tradition, of the different states in which mankind have really lived. Before all property was engrossed by the few, all had sufficient to supply their wants—this was the golden age: to supply which wants is now the cause of all care—this is the iron age.

Where there is a sufficiency to supply the ordinary wants of human nature, and where that supply is certain, and we are confident that there is no danger of its failing, the source of all care and solicitude is cut off; even losses and accidents, all lose their power of sensibly affecting us, when this is the case; and which would be the case if the lower orders of the people were put in a plentiful and comfortable state. This a good government has the power of effecting, by taking care that none of the people become so powerful as to oppress their fellow subjects, either in the open and more evident manner, as feudal lords do their vassals; or in the indirect and masked one, by the means of great and unequal property.

In addition therefore to such considerations as arise from justice, humanity, and the principle of doing to others as we would be done by, the self-interested motive, of removing or lessening an evil to which we ourselves are exposed, might induce us to better the condition of the poor, in order to render that situation comfortable to which the wealthiest may be reduced. By so doing, we not only guard against the fatal contingency, but we render our present enjoyments, whatever they may be, comfortable and complete, by removing that which embitters and renders them hollow and unsatisfactory—the reflection on the uncertainty of their continuance.

The system of civilization, as it is very improperly called, has not only ill effects on the greatest part of individulals composing

posing a state, but also on the state itself, taken as a collected body; which, contrary to the received opinion, it weakens, impoverishes, and renders truly more barbarous.—We are next, therefore, to consider the effects of civilization on states or nations.

## SECTION XIX.

### MANUFACTURES THE CAUSE AND SIGN OF THE POVERTY OF NATIONS.

It has been seen that a very large majority of the people, in most civilized states, are in the class of the poor; but if the individuals, composing almost the whole of the collected body, are poor, how can the nation be said to be rich? Manufacturing states appear to other nations, and they persuade themselves so too, that they are very wealthy. There appear in many distant ports numbers of their ships, loaded with valuable goods of

every

every kind ; and in the same manner they are seen in their own ports. But this seems to me to indicate directly the contrary. The great quantities of manufactured goods suppose a great number of manufacturers, who, if they were not poor, would not submit to the employments that produce them. The manufactures being brought together in large quantities, in ships, in warehouses, and in shops, are put more in view ; but this only shows that there are certain rich men, who, commanding the labours of many, can collect great magazines of their works ; allowing them a small pittance for their own and their families subsistence. If we see great quantities of honey, should we think the bees, from whom it was taken, rich and well stored with that which they subsist on ?

That country is considered by many as the richest, which abounds most in such things as are generally looked upon as composing wealth ; and the means, in their opinions, to make a country rich, is to make of the people as many manufacturers as can be made ; and to force

these

those to turn out as many manufactured goods as possible; and that these manufactured things shall be of that kind of which the manufacturers themselves shall consume the least possible quantity.

But that might, with much more justice, be called the poorest country that can be found, since the great bulk of the people have as little as they can possibly be subsisted on.

When, therefore, we talk of the riches, and flourishing state of the manufacturing countries, we should limit our representations to the few who enjoy the productions of the manufactures; and not extend them to those who labour in producing them.

Monsieur Brissot, in his travels through North America, tells us, that he went to see a piece of curious machinery made by Mr. Pope, of New-York, who said he should be glad to dipose of it; but added, that they were poor people in America, and there was no person who could afford to buy it. On which M. Brissot observes, that though there was no person rich enough there to purchase the instrument, yet it was no proof that they were a poor people: it only proved that property was more equally divided; and that no great accumulation was in any one person's hands.

We have shown that it is one principal property in refined manufactures to render the works of the poor man more consumable; and that they actually give occasion to the rich of making greater waste than would otherwise be possible: how, then, can they possibly have any other effect than to impoverish? That system which produces most things that are useful and necessary, and that system too that employs the most frugality in the use of them, and makes them extend furthest, is that which must enrich most.

It may be objected, that in Ireland, where there are few manufactures, the situation of the poor is even worse than it is in manufacturing states. I admit that it is. This does not, however, in the least disprove what I have said concerning the effects of manufactures. We read in that very able work, the Dissertation

tion of Dr. Crump, to which the prize was adjudged by the Irish Academy, that a very large part of the lands in Ireland was obtained by greedy courtiers, on the occasion of confiscations, after the many conquests that have taken place in that unfortunate island: that these lands are now possessed in a great measure by absentees and other great proprietors: that they in general let them in large portions to persons who let them again to others, and these again to the farmers who occupy them: that these men, who are called middle men, all get a profit rent, and live by sucking the blood of the farmer: that the farmers there, contrary to what happens in England, do not think it necessary to have a capital for the occupation of a farm, but frequently take a large one without any; parts of which they let out again, divided among others as poor as themselves, who have no other means of cultivating them than by their own and family's labour with the spade; a plough being often not to be found in a large district; and when it is, it frequently belongs to the maker, who lets it out to

hire,

hire, at an extravagant price. These miserable farmers, having no capital to lay out in labour, can employ few or no husbandmen; the poor, therefore, can earn little or nothing, either by manufactures, or labouring in the field. The renters who have capitals are graziers, and require few hands. By this arrangement, the same effect is produced as by the manufacturing system, viz. the preventing the poor from working on the land, and at the coarser trades, and by that means producing for themselves the necessaries of life. And this is equally the effect of the wealth of rich individuals, who spend most of their incomes in the refined manufactures, though these are not the produce of Ireland.

Hence the poor, by earning little either by manufactures or labouring in the field, have little or nothing to lay out in the purchase of the necessaries of life, i. e. the produce of the land. This produce, therefore, is almost wholly exported. Their lean cattle are sent to all the ports of the western coast of England, Bristol channel, &c. to be fed by the English graziers, through-

throughout the whole kingdom; their fat cattle are slaughtered to victual the English ships of war and merchant ships, and also for the consumption of the inhabitants of their sea-coast, and of many other parts of the world; their butter, tallow, skins, are in great part exported: and the money arising from all these things sent to the absentees and others, for rent and tithes. Thus the inhabitants of the country are almost wholly deprived of the produce of the land they inhabit; and they live, if they can be said to live, on a very small part of it, by raising potatoes in corners of fields and other small unoccupied places. And here let me ask the lawyer, civilian, or divine, whether the inhabitants of a country have not a right to make use of the produce of it for their subsistence*; and whether any human

* It might also be asked, whether, if the proprietors of land have a right to export out of the country, the articles of subsistence above-mentioned, they have not a right, too, to refuse the poor the corners of their fields to cultivate potatoes: and thus to deprive them of all sustenance.

laws

laws or power can justly prevent them from doing it.

"Behold," says Dr. Crump, "an Irish "farmer going forth to his work, barefoot, "covered with rags; behold his ruinous "hovel, built of mud, covered with weeds, "and pervious to every shower that falls, "every pinching gale that blows; behold "him seated, after his hard labour, sur-"rounded by naked children, sharing "with them his dry and scanty meal." Thousands have no house at all to live in—but, as was observed by a member of a great assembly, a few winters ago, are seen huddling together under bridges, arch-ways, ricks, and in any place where a shelter over head can be had.

## SECTION XX.

### CIVILIZATION AND MANUFACTURES RENDER A NATION MORE IGNORANT AND BARBAROUS.

Nor are the boastings of civilized countries, with respect to learning, better founded. Certain individuals are learned: but what is the mass of the people? If we average the learning of any of these countries, it is greatly exceeded by the savages of North America; who clearly show, by their speeches on public embassies, and their debates in their assemblies at home, that they have availed themselves of the leisure they enjoy; but which is refused European artificers. Learning, in the unequal shares it is distributed among individuals in Europe, is clearly prejudicial; giving some an unfair advantage over others of their fellow creatures. It is the chief instrument by which the superiority is gained by the

few

few over the many; and by which the latter are kept in subjection. It is like the turning a game cock, with steel spurs, among those who have only their natural weapons.

The bulk of the people are not only ignorant themselves, but derive very few advantages from the learning of others. The three learned professions *, for instance, benefit them in a very small degree. As to the law, the subject of this is property, of which they have none. With respect to physic, it has been doubted whether the practice of the art is really beneficial or not to mankind. The practice of medicine in the hands of a person who has acquired the sciences preparatory to the study of it; and, after that, has had and availed himself of the opportunities of acquiring the science itself, and the practical part; who withal has a sound and penetrating understanding; is of a sober and cautious way of thinking and acting; and, above all, of strict and disinterested probity; such a man, enjoy-

* See Note S.

ing this rare assemblage of talents and attainments, may certainly be of service to his fellow creatures: but how few such are there in the number that practise! In the present state of matters, very few physicians have been so educated; and of the great body of practitioners none at all. There is no doubt but that the mischief done in practice exceeds the benefit. But whatever advantage the wealthy may receive, who are generally attended with a diligence proportionable to their abilities of paying for it, it cannot be a doubt whether or no the slight attention paid to the cases of the poor, and the few visits they are able to pay for, can be of any service to them.

With regard to what advantage the poor derive from the profession of divinity, that has already been briefly considered.

It has been said, that, by the encouragement given the arts and sciences, discoveries are made, as in chemistry and mechanics, which are beneficial to mankind: but these discoveries generally concern the fine arts and manufactures, from which few advantages, but many disadvantages, descend to the lower orders. As to machinery introduced in the manufactures, to abridge labour, whatever use this might be of, if otherwise employed, as it is, it is rarely of any; a greater degree of refinement being required in proportion as the labour is lessened: so that on the whole the labour of the manufacturers is not diminished, but rendered, as we have shown before, more tedious, more dangerous, more injurious to them. Nor is more of the labour of the poor employed in furnishing such things as they themselves make use of, than before such discoveries.

Whatever discoveries are made, it falls to their lot to put them in execution—not to enjoy the fruits of them. The improvements in astronomy have facilitated navigation. The consequence of this has been to throw more men on the sea, that unnatural element to man, and to expose them to all the hardships attending it; but to receive very little of the luxuries introduced by it—as has been before demonstrated.

Mr. Hume having ascribed very different effects to civilization, it seems proper to take some notice of what so eminent a writer has said on the subject.

In his Essay on Refinement in the Arts, after stating that happiness seems to consist of three ingredients, viz. action, pleasure, and indolence, he says,

That these refinements furnish a fund for conversation, and by these means promote sociability.

That they refine our pleasures, and by so doing lessen the grosser excesses, as drunkenness, &c.

That they multiply our gratifications.

That they soften our manners, and promote moderation.

It is obvious that all this is said, and intended to be understood, as applicable only to those who enjoy the effects or produce of the refined arts; not to those who by their labour furnish them: or, in other words, all this is said of the rich, and is therefore not inconsistent with what I have advanced. But it must be allowed

to

to be a very partial representation of the effects of the arts. This is constantly the case with all the panegyrists of them. The poor, although the bulk of the people, are always kept out of sight, and every thing which regards them passed over in their splendid descriptions. The truth is, the arts have raised a few, both in respect of their intellectual attainments and their enjoyments, above the natural state of man: but, in order to obtain those advantages for those few, they have sunk the remainder of the people much below it.

Lord Chesterfield has observed, that in history we read of nobody but kings, lords, bishops, generals, &c. as if they composed all mankind, or that the rest was not worth notice.

# SECTION XXI.

## CIVILIZATION AND MANUFACTURES WEAKEN A NATION.

THEY as little contribute to strengthen a nation. It has been shown that they directly tend to lessen the number of the people, which is ever in proportion to their subsistence; and this we have seen is greatly diminished by the manufactures; and cannot, as has also been demonstrated, be replaced by importations: they also debase the species: they lessen the stature of man: they misshape his body: they enervate, and diminish his strength and activity, and his ability to bear hardships: and with all these effects on his body, they depress the spirit and vigour of his mind, and thus, in every respect, unfit him for war.

Civilization operates in another manner in weakening a country. The great phenomenon in a civilized nation, is the inequality

inequality of property in it. The wealth of all kinds being in a few hands, all the others are destitute of it; by which means these have little interest in the defence of it. If every man had an allotment of land, had his patrimony, his inheritance, every man would fight bravely, expose himself to the greatest danger, to maintain his stake. The mode of fighting by mercenaries, in modern tactics, is chiefly by cannonading and firing at a distance; they seldom engage hand to hand, with the point of the bayonet or the sword; this requires a resolution which mercenaries seldom have. The leaders of armies, apprehensive of this, adopt the present method, where the contest is generally determined by the superior skill in the engineer. To urge men to rush on the point of the bayonet, or to stand an attack of that kind, when resolutely made, they must have something to lose more valuable, in their estimation, than their lives. This can only be a freehold; that which supports them, their wives, and children; to lose which would truly be a greater loss than that of their lives.

An instance of this happened lately in Switzerland *, where an army of 30,000 of the best troops in France, the conquerors of all Europe, could not withstand the impetuous attack of less than the one-sixth part of their own number, of half-armed, half-disciplined freeholders. It is not the numbers of an army, or their discipline, that conquers, except they are on both sides mercenaries, brought into the field to fight the cause of other people, in which they themselves have no interest. A few men, such as the Swiss were, are formidable to the largest armies.

In a system contrary to that of civilization, the number of robust, warlike men, would be much increased, perhaps doubled in a few years. Having the same extent of country to defend, these men too might be disciplined from their youth; for there would then be no danger attend the putting arms into their hands.

And is there no necessity, to speak of England in particular, on this occasion,

* See "The History of the Invasion of Switzerland, by Henry Zschokke, National Prefect of the Canton of Basil," 1803, Longman, &c.

for

for our attempting to increase our means of defence? France, it is highly probable, will soon be an over-match for us by sea, as it already is by land. The immense tract of sea-coast it has, will furnish it with more sailors than we have. The circumstance of our having more ships, at present, than France, is not to be reckoned on; for all these will be destroyed, in fifteen years hence, by the ordinary course of decay: so that it is nearly as easy for the French to build a new navy, as it is for us to keep up our's; which must be all built over again in that space of time: not to mention the uncertain defence maritime force affords.

Historians have universally observed, that wealth, and its attendant, luxury, have constantly preceded the decline and fall of states. Taking this fact as admitted, it is easily seen, from the principles laid down in this Treatise, in what manner the destruction of empires is brought about. In a wealthy and luxurious nation, the people are principally divided into two classes, namely, the opulent and the indigent. These latter are either

labourers

labourers or mechanics. The middle rank of people, viz. the small proprietors of land, and lesser farmers, compose a very small body of the people. It is from these, almost only, that a healthy race of people are to be raised: but even these are not of the robust nature, stature, &c. which they would have been, if they had not lived so much on salted provisions as they do; being tempted by the prices the rich give for the other products of their farms. The offspring of the rich are frequently observed to be degenerated in all the qualities of mind and body. We have seen the same effects happen to the poor, from the other and opposite causes. On these several accounts, a wealthy and luxurious people are ill qualified to defend themselves against any power that invades them: at the same time that this wealth, i. e. the articles of luxury, i. e. again the refined manufactures, are a strong temptation to the less effeminate and corrupted, or more adventurous neighbours, to invade them.

The fall of wealthy states also frequently happens

happens from internal and domestic convulsions, which is equally explainable on my principles.

Most civilized states, in which the wealthy part i. e. those having the power of the nation in their hands, being few in number in comparison with the rest of the people, are obliged, as has been seen, to keep large standing armies of mercenary troops, to hold the people, who are so much superior in numbers to themselves, in subjection. This body of troops, induced as has been before explained, have often subjected the people, together with their masters, and proved the destruction of the state. The revolution in the Roman republic was effected in the latter manner, by the soldiery under Julius Cæsar. The state under the Emperors was overturned in the former manner by the invasion of the Goths and Vandals.

It was the manufactures of India that attracted the visits of Europeans, and also enabled them, though in such small numbers, to subdue and pillage that numerous people.

Thus

Thus the system of manufacturing operates, in both these manners, to weaken and destroy states.

## SECTION XXII.

### THAT THE POOR CONTRIBUTE MOST TO MOST GOVERNMENTS.

ALTHOUGH the poor enjoy so few advantages, or rather suffer so many deprivations and hardships, in the present state of things in most civilized nations; yet they contribute infinitely more to the defence of their respective governments than the other class. They fight the battles by sea and land, to do which many of them are torn from their houses, their wives and their children, and undergo every kind of suffering that human nature can be afflicted with.

With respect to those who serve in the navies, they most frequently are dragged forcibly on board ships of war; the militias

tias or conscripts, also, of most countries *, for the most part serve by compulsion; and as to the regular, or enlisted, every art is generally used to draw them into the service.

The poor, in most civilized nations, not only supply the men that make up the armies, but their hands furnish every necessary for the men, when embodied, to carry on the war †. This will appear by

* With respect to the militias of most countries, I cannot help observing that, if a poor man is drawn, he must inevitably go; or, if the man has a little property, be obliged to give half or the whole to be excused: but the rich man is excused for perhaps the fifty-thousandth part of his property—a sum perhaps not equal to his current expenses for one hour. The sum to be proportioned to the substance of the person drawn, should be a proportionable part of the whole, as a half, a fourth, a tenth, a hundredth; and not a certain sum, which to one man may be his whole, or a half—to another not the ten-thousandth part.

† "As the use of money was unknown, all taxes were paid in kind; and thus not only the natural productions of all the different provinces of the empire, but every species of manufacture, and every work of ingenuity and art, were collected in the public storehouses: from those, the Emperor supplied his numerous train of attendants in peace, and his armies in time of war, with food, with clothes, and ornaments. People of inferior condition, neither possessing land, nor engaged in commerce, were bound to the performance of various services." —Robertson's History of America, vol. iii. p. 173.

shortly

shortly enumerating those things, viz. provisions, clothes, arms, ammunition, &c. &c. Every article in these different kinds is produced by the labour of the poor, and with the effect of reducing the quantity of their meals and clothing. Their labour, which produces all these things, being taken from raising the corn and potatoes, which their meals consist of, lessens the meals just in the same degree as if they had been directly taken from off the plates and dishes out of which they were eating. This part, therefore, of the support of most civilized nations, i. e. against external enemies, is ultimately born by the poor, to the very great increase of their wants and sufferings. War operates in a twofold manner; first, by taking off the men the army consists of from agriculture; and then, by occasioning the necessity of supplying these men with provisions, clothes, &c. It is evident, without further illustration, that the internal expenses of most states are born by the poor in the same manner, and with the same consequences, of increasing their distress. We have seen that all the salaries,

ries, revenues, taxes, &c. are ultimately paid with such things as the labour of the poor has furnished.

It is to be feared that these wars, of which the poor bear the burden, and in which millions of them lose their limbs, their health, and their lives, are often entered into for the express purpose of increasing their subjection and oppression, and making them the instruments of it. It is highly probable, for instance, that wars have been concerted privately, and undertaken by neighbouring kings, for the sole purpose of gaining a pretence for increasing their forces, and keeping up a larger standing army; the chief view in augmenting which was to keep their own people in closer subjection, and lay and enforce further restraints and impositions on them. If there should be some people who will not allow of this highly probable supposition; yet all must allow that wars are often begun on slight pretences; the real views being as above represented.

And if the true motives, which induced most of the powers to engage their people in the last war, were to be avowed; it

would

would appear that they arose from their apprehensions that the people would recover some of their natural and just rights, and obtain some little melioration of their condition. It was then thought that the French people were endeavouring to recover not only the equality of rights, in the sense it was explained; but that they had in view to lessen somewhat the great inequality of property also: both these ideas were comprehended, as it was thought, under the term of French principles. To prevent their succeeding in which, and the contagion which it was supposed would have followed their success, was the object, perhaps, principally aimed at. This, I believe, discovers more of the design of the war, and who were the aggressors, than all that Mr. Herbert Marsh, in his laboured volumes, has said. This was the real cause why the ministers of most of the states found every thing they proposed so readily adopted by the aristocratical part of their respective countries, and which enabled them to carry and force down measures so abhorrent to what had ever before, though often proposed, been acceded to.

If these conjectures are true, how are the poor to be pitied! The reflection that all the calamities of the poor originated from, and were really the works of, *men's hands;* that fresh calamities have been purposely brought on them; and that they themselves have been made use of as instruments to confirm their old grievances, add to, and perpetuate them; is too sad for a human heart to dwell on.

---

## SECTION XXIII.

### THE CAUSE OF THE FREQUENCY OF WARS.

THE burden thus falling on the lower order of people, (for the number of the other order in armies, in proportion, is trifling, and those few have such advantages in them as to make it an object of choice

choice with them)—the hardship, I say, thus falling almost solely on the poor, it is not to be wondered at, that we hear the wealthy talk of and propose war with all the unconcern and indifference they do.

It has always seemed, notwithstanding, a matter of surprise, that in the present enlightened age such a destructive calamity should be suffered to be brought so often, by a few persons, on a whole people; and that it must have some peculiar cause that occasions it: for, if the lights we receive from reason and morality, or the feelings of human nature, had been suffered to influence us, I think it would have been long since that this horrid monster would have been driven from the land.

Without inquiring into this preternatural cause at present, I shall proceed to observe, that wealth, which seems to be the cause of so many other evils of human life, is also a principal cause of this worst of all calamities.

Wealth putting it in the power of its possessors to give great prices for such things as they are desirous of having, viz.

the

the articles of their luxurious tables, their costly furniture, dress, plate, jewels, &c. the whole world is ransacked for them; no part of the globe is left unexplored in order to obtain them *.

The rich of most of the different civilized nations of Europe, all coveting the same things, the countries producing those things are the continual objects of contests and wars between these different powers. These wars are easily excited by the rich, who are either themselves the persons with whom lies the power of making war and peace; or are the persons who have great influence with those who have that power.

These are the chief motives on which foreign and other conquests are attempted, and of course of most of the wars of modern times. If property was equally divided, and there were no rich, the inhabitants of a parish would seldom be led out of their parish for any thing wanted; every place would produce every thing that there was a real occasion for.

* Vide Note R.

The objects of all wars, whether near or distant, are to increase trade, or to extend territory; or the wars are occasioned by the ambition or irritability of the rich. As to the first cause: although the wars, entered into on this account, are often said to be undertaken for the benefit of the people, they have really no other effect than the obtaining the insignificant things above mentioned. As to the second object: this is desired only by the aggressors, in order to place a greater number of people, the inhabitants of their intended new acquisitions, under their subjection; whose labour they may employ to the same purposes that they do that of the poor of their own country.

With respect to the third cause: we have said that the inequality of property or wealth puts the power and command over the people into the hands of the few, who can call them out into the field at any time; and thus the making war is facilitated; it also disposes the *few* to engage in them. Those who have this power are rendered by it arrogant, quick of resentment,

ment, vain, and fond of showing that power. The slightest causes therefore are sufficient to incite such men to war. Whereas, were the people themselves, who bear the burden of the war, and who would gain no object, but great loss, whatever the success might be, to be the persons by whom it was to be determined, whether there should be war or peace, we should have few wars.

The authors, therefore, of all wars are the wealthy; and the objects of them, an increase of wealth. Wealth, i.e. inequality of property, therefore, in both *cases*, is the cause of almost all wars.

The education given by the rich to their children, is calculated to give them a warlike spirit, that is, to enflame them with the desire of bloodshed. The books they read treat of little else than of heros and the exploits of heros, that is, of bloody warriors, and bloody wars. The most destructive battles are called splendid, brilliant, glorious; and such other extravagant epithets are made use of, as might well be called ridiculous, if they were not

artfully

artfully designed to cover and disguise their baneful effects. We seldom have any account given of the horrid spectacles to be found in the field, the day after the battle—the mangled carcasses, dying groans, and heaps of the dead—or the hospitals full of wounded, diseased, and dying men.

It might be said that wars are as frequent among barbarous nations as among civilized people. They certainly happen among them; but are, I believe, not so frequent. They arise from causes in some respects similar, in both. Savages subsist on the game they get by hunting. In pursuing it, they are often carried almost necessarily into the districts of neighbouring nations; which intrusions, often involuntary, are almost always, at least generally, the causes of wars with them. It must be allowed that the Indians, in going to war for the necessaries of life, act much more rationally than the polished nations, who go to war for such baubles and trinkets, and in doing which they greatly diminish the necessaries of life. It will be seen that, in the middle state, described

in

in the sequel, that this great evil, attending the both extremes of society, would probably be altogether, or in a great measure, avoided.

---

## SECTION XXIV.

### ON NATIONAL DEBTS.

One great effect of war being to occasion and increase the debt of the nation engaged in it, and this contributing greatly to put the poor of most civilized countries in the situation in which they are, renders it a subject proper to be here considered.

Various have been the opinions with regard to the effects of a public debt; some auguring the worst consequences from it; others considering it as of an indifferent nature, or even expecting beneficial consequences from it: but these opinions have been founded on conjectures and hypothesis; not on an accurate knowledge

ledge of its nature, and of its necessary tendency.

A public debt is to be considered in two views: as due to foreigners, and as due to the subjects of the indebted nation. These two sorts have been considered as of very different natures: that of the former, as sending out of the indebted kingdom so much wealth annually as the dividends amount to, and therefore very hurtful to it: that of the latter has been thought by many as of no detriment to the nation; since, in their opinion, it only removes property from one set of subjects to another; the wealth still remaining in the kingdom.

I imagine this distinction is not just. To the subject of the indebted nation, as well as the foreigner, the interest is paid ultimately with the produce of the labour of the poor, viz. in part that of the husbandman, and in part that of the manufacturer; and being consumed by the subject as well as the foreign creditor, it is entirely, with respect to the nation, the same thing; for, if the stock the foreigner had, were to become the property of a subject

bject, a consumption equal to the interest would take place in the same manner. Whether any advantage follows from the subject's money being spent within his own, i. e. the indebted nation, may be known from the principles already laid down.

But the debt of a nation has an effect not considered by any one. It creates a new and additional species of wealth, or a new claim on the people—or, in other words, it is a fresh power created and given to a new and additional set of men, (the holders of stock) over the labouring people. To pay the interest of the debt, new taxes are laid on. All these taxes are every where ultimately paid with the produce of the labour of the poor: for with what else than that can the public levies be paid *? With the money paid these new creditors, they procure the commodities which they consume; and in the end it is just the same thing as if they were first paid in kind. A stockholder, therefore, is another person added to the al-

* Vide Note, p. 164.

ready great multitude of unproductive consumers. Hence more of the produce of the labour of the poor is taken from them; and of course still less is left behind for their own use. So that war not only occasions an additional consumption of the produce of the labour of the poor, during its continuance, equal to the amount of the loan, and other expenditures; but raises and leaves a permanent body of unproductive and most wasteful consumers to exist for ever after. What other effects war produces, such as the increasing the number of supporters of government, I shall here take no notice of.

Hence, by war, the poor, the bulk of all armies, after being exposed to all the dangers of it, being worse accommodated in the field, and, when hurt and wounded, taken less care of; after all their own sufferings, and after the want and distress of their relations, occasioned by their absence; instead of having their situation bettered, find it worse on their return; both good and ill success operating to their disadvantage: for if we suppose, in

the

the former event, the acquisition of a new sugar or a spice island, the produce of it only stimulates the rich, now increased in number, to send out of the land more of the necessaries of life, (which, as we have shown, all exports are, and which are so sorely wanted by the poor natives) to purchase and bring back that produce for their own consumption solely.

But a question arises---what effect the paying off this public debt would have on the mass of the people? In answer to this question, it must be observed,

That the principal money, which would be paid the public creditor, would be retained and preserved by him; would not become extinct; it would only suffer a transfer, and continue to be what it was before, to wit, a claim on the labour of the poor, to the same or nearly the same amount as before. If it was otherwise, that is, if the claim on the labour of the poor ceased, the public creditor, on receiving his money, would receive nothing; for it would be nothing to him, if it did not command, as before, the labour of the poor. But it is evident that his money would

would procure the same things as before, and which would be furnished by the hands of the poor, as before. He would preserve his claim; and the labouring part of the people must answer that claim: they would therefore, in no degree, be relieved from the burden of the public debts by the payment; but, on the contrary, it would, perhaps, bring an additional weight to be supported by them; for, in order to pay off this public debt, fresh taxes must be laid on, or there must be a continuation of those already in being, for a longer time than would be otherwise necessary. As far, therefore, as any of these taxes would bear on the poor, so far their burden would receive an additional weight.

But with respect to the rich, they would be really eased of part of their burden, and that part would bear a proportion to the portion of the public debt that should be paid off by taxes levied on the labouring class of the people. The rich would be really benefited, but it would be at the expense of the poor.

## SECTION XXV.

### ON PRIVILEGED ORDERS, AS ESTABLISHED IN MOST CIVILIZED STATES.

PRIVILEGED orders are found only in civilized states; being therefore peculiar to them, they may be thought a part of my subject: little, however, seems necessary to be said, as privileges are very nearly related to riches; and, having almost the same effects, are liable to the same objections.

Privileges are of several kinds, such, viz. as convey honours, power, or profit. The first are in themselves innocent; and only hurtful, when given as a reward for actions undeserving them—as for victories in unnecessary wars, &c. It is, however, to be remembered, that dignities, titles, and all kinds of honours, place the subjects of them in their distinguished situations, rather by depressing other people, than by raising them.

The second kind may be useful in the present state of things. Some species of power

power may be necessary; but perhaps it is only in the present state that it is so: in the extremely unequal division of property, where the bulk of the people are stripped of every degree of it; where they are deprived of every gratification enjoyed by the rich, and reduced to such things as have the effect of merely supporting life, without imparting any of the enjoyments of it. The things, however, which afford gratifications and enjoyments to human nature, though they have none themselves, they see abundantly possessed and profusely wasted by the rich, and have by that means their desires and longings strongly excited. In such state of things, and in order to preserve them in that state, power must be lodged in certain persons' hands; and this power must be very great; it must be irresistible. To keep people that are cold, naked, and hungry, from taking fuel to warm themselves, clothes to cover themselves with, and food to satisfy their hunger; when plenty of all those things are before their eyes; to prevent such people from taking these things requires a magistracy armed with powers indeed; they must have a power of inflicting punishments greater than the sufferings of the poor; which, as these sufferings are continual and unremitting, it is not easy to invent. Those can be nothing short of torments and death, and even these will be found unequal to the occasion. But the necessity of committing this great power to any one, is a necessity created by the present system of things in most civilized states. It is, notwithstanding, unnatural to arm one human creature against another. We do not see lions armed against lions; nor tigers against tigers.

> Indica tigris agit rabida cum tigride pacem
> Perpetuam; sævis inter se convenit ursis. Juv.

The taking away the life of a man by another man is an unnatural action, at which the common feelings of mankind revolt. If any act of man can be deemed wicked, it is this: to justify, therefore, such an act, and render the author of it innocent, many have thought that reasons should be assigned, founded on the clearest, soundest, and most indubitable principles:

principles: grounded on the common sense, common sentiments, and universal assent of mankind. Whether the laws inflicting capital punishments in all civilized nations are thus founded; and whether the persons that make such laws are vested with a real power of taking away the lives of men; I shall not take upon me to discuss.

The third kind of privileges may be again divided into two species: either such as immediately give wealth, as ecclesiastical benefices and preferments, commissions in armies and navies, places under governments, and numberless other places, pensions, &c.; or such as put privileged persons in the way of acquiring wealth, as, the profession of law, lucrative contracts, &c. All these, furnishing the means of making rich men, have the same objections lying against them as may be made against wealth itself, as well with regard to the origin as the effects of them. It should be remembered, that it cannot be given to one without taking it from another.

## SECTION XXVI.

### ON POWER.

We have endeavoured, in a former chapter, to show that wealth is a certain species of power; viz. a power over the labour of the poor. We have further endeavoured to show, that it is the source of all power exercised in civilized governments. As this power, therefore, is so great an agent in most civilized nations, and as the state of civilization differs in nothing more from the opposite state, than in this particular matter, we shall consider power more generally.

By power, we mean that authority which is exercised by man over man; it may, therefore, be called human power; both its agent and the subject of the action being man.

This power disposes of the lives and fortunes of men. It inflicts punishments; commands and directs the labour of men, and takes the produce of it.

The

The foundation of power may be of three kinds, viz.

1st, Power (in one person or a few) may be supported on the opinion of the people.

2dly, Power may be supported by the force of arms in the hands of part of the people; i. e. by a military government.

3dly, Power may be supported by the medium of wealth.

It is easy to be conceived how the first two species of power are raised. The third species of power is raised by the seizure or assumption (by one or a few persons) of all the land, and other things arising from it, in which the necessaries of life are included; and of which, in order to obtain a sufficient quantity to sustain their existence, the people must submit to such services and labour as those, who are in possession of them, require; i. e. must be subject to them.

This last species, namely, that supported by wealth, is that which some modern nations are governed by; whether monarchical, republican, &c.: for, the most absolute monarch, not being supported by one

one or other of the two first methods, and not finding the lands in the hands of an aristocracy; in order to sustain his authority, has no other means than to take, from the people at large, the land, &c. &c. and to give them to certain people, part of the great mass; who, in order to secure to themselves what is thus put in their possession, will support him in his authority: it is, therefore, a government supported by wealth in the hands of a few, and is, in fact, an aristocracy, as we have before observed; differing only from other aristocracies, in having its head a little more exalted than the rest.

Power acquired and supported by this last means, is perhaps the least eligible to the people, for three reasons: 1st, because it is most expensive; 2dly, because it is seldom affectionate and in their interest; and, 3dly, because it is the most difficult to be shaken off, in case of maladministration.

1st, As to expensiveness: The monarch, whose authority depends on the opinion of the people, whether that opinion is founded on his virtue, wisdom, or prowess,

or

or on his imaginary right by birth, only requires from the people what is necessary to furnish the pleasures, the splendor, and the hospitality of one man, and a small number of such others as are connected with him by the ties of real friendship. The expense of this, to the whole people, is insignificant.

The expense attending a monarch whose authority is supported by a standing army, is greater than the last; it is not, however, large; his army being mere soldiers, who live by their profession; rising up daily out of the people; and, being not men of rank and fortune, and paid at the rate of mercenery troops, generally perhaps a little above the rate of the wages for the labour of the people; living in idleness, and exempt from hardship, the greater part of their time; and being therefore satisfied with this; the expense of one hundred thousand such men, to a people consisting of ten or twelve millions, would not be above the one-twentieth or thirtieth part of the amount of the labour of the people. Or, if you suppose that ten or twelve millions of people will turn

out

out two millions of working hands, it would not require more than one half an hour, of eight or ten hours labour in the day, to support it.

Where the sovereign authority* is supported by the power of wealth, the land being taken away from the people, and also almost the whole produce of their labour, i. e. almost the whole of their property, (these two comprising the whole of it) the part returned to them being, as has been before shown, not above one-ninth of it; the expense to the people, for the charges of government, amounts to a great proportion of what they have: so that the people actually give that proportion of their property and labour to be governed.

2dly, A government supported by wealth is seldom affectionate and in the interest of the people. When the sovereign is the choice of the people, selected by them for his superior qualities, it is probable that some degree at least of re-

* In almost all civilized states, the wealthy, i. e. the aristocracy, make use of an army as means to support their power; though, for distinction sake, we have considered the matter as above.

ciprocal

ciprocal affection must take place: there are very few dispositions in which it would not: the natural temper of some of the monarchs, at least, would be good; some men are naturally kind, humane, compassionate, and grateful: whenever these good dispositions occurred, the people would feel the good effects of them: but where wealth rules in the abstract, as it were, from thence what are we to expect? Trade knows no friends or kindred—Avarice no compassion—Gain no bounds.

3dly, A government that is supported by the assumption of the wealth of a nation into the hands of the few, is objectionable because, if found oppressive or injurious to the people, it is most difficultly removed. The principal part of the wealth of the whole nation being in possession of, perhaps, one eighth or tenth of the people; who, with the superior knowledge their education gives them, in all the arts necessary for the purpose; with the means of deluding, bribing, decoying, and compelling the common people to serve by requisition; with the power of rendering themselves the legislators

lators exclusively, and of making every step taken by their opponents illegal and punishable with death: in fine, by being in the possession of the arms, fortresses, &c. &c. their number is sufficient to keep under their subjection the rest of the people, though so much exceeding their own numbers; and this they may do till they have carried their oppression to a certain degree which cannot be born by the people.

It happens that unanimity and agreement are preserved amongst the opulent, and jealousies and disagreement prevented in a manner that would not be expected in a mass of people so very discordant in many respects. This discordance arises from the great difference in the degree of wealth, and from many of them living and preying on others of them; and holding invidious superiorities, and controlling powers &c. This agreement, notwithstanding those obstacles, is occasioned by the reflection which every one of them makes, that though there be a great difference in their conditions, yet still the condition of the least of them is abundantly better

better than that of the people; that it gives them a comfortable sufficiency and independence; that the assurance and preservation of this situation depends on the integrity and intirety of the whole body. He therefore cordially unites in his endeavours to preserve the great body of his party, and its interests, intire; which by union only can subsist, and the condition, advantage, and privileges of each individual of it be continued. Conscious of the advantages they assume over the people, they consider themselves as looked upon as enemies by them, who must, therefore, they think, be waiting for opportunities of reclaiming what they esteem their rights: and the seeing them at the doors in such superior numbers to themselves is a further motive for their strict union; as, on the aggression of foreign enemies, domestic feuds and political contentions cease.

# SECTION XXVII.

## ON NATIONAL REVENUES.

These are only to be found in civilized states, and therefore require to be treated of here. I have, notwithstanding, on this subject little more to say, than to correct that which seems to me to be an erroneous idea entertained by the public in most civilized states. In order to do this, it might be necessary to consider what a revenue is.

A revenue then is, in the first instance, a sum of money collected from the people and paid into the public treasury annually. It has been observed before, that, though the money seems to be the subject-matter of the revenue, it is not such in effect: for, in the first place, in order to procure this money, commodities of various kinds, as those of the produce of the lands, of the manufactures, &c. are raised and sold; and the money, when paid to government,

government, before the exigencies of state can be supplied, must again be changed into the very articles, or some such as have been sold, to procure that money; for example, the beef, pork, corn, wool, &c. that the farmer sold to raise the money that was paid by him or his landlord for taxes, must be bought again with the money, before the ships of war can be victualled, armies clothed, &c. The use of money in this case *, only prevents the necessity of carrying the things from the place where they are raised, to the place where they are consumed. But this matter has been explained before. A revenue therefore consists of articles collected from the people, to be applied to the use the public service requires. Now what are those articles? The general answer to this question is, that they are the things that the labour of the people has produced; and that of course they must be collected, directly or indirectly, from the poor, before they can make a part of the revenue

* Vide Note, p. 164.

This

This is a plain, and I believe, just account, or idea, of what a revenue, or, as it is called, resources, of a country are; for want of which, what has generally been said concerning them, has been hardly intelligible; and has given occasion to such different and opposite opinions relating to the state of them.

The intention of all we have to say is to caution politicians against relying too much on the power and resources of their respective nations, and, depending on these, leading them imprudently into wars, schemes of commerce, and other such projects.

The great object of triumph with most powers is the increasing state of their revenues: and the grand object of their attention is the continuance of them. To this idol is sacrificed every thing. To it are devoted the lives of the people in a thousand different ways. If the West-India islands destroy thousands and ten thousands of soldiers; if misery and slavery are entailed on millions of our fellow creatures; it must be suffered, it is said, for the sugar brings in a great sum to the revenues.

revenues. If the distillers convert a substance, that is a most wholesome food, into a most pernicious poison; it must be suffered, because it brings in large sums to the revenues.

And what is this great subject of national joy, triumph, and confidence? Is it really an increase of those articles which constitute substantial and beneficial wealth?

The increase of revenues arises from two sources: the one from the increase of those things which pay a duty, excise, &c. whether they are consumed at the places where they are raised, or are exported or imported; the other from the increase of taxes and other impositions. With respect to the former, we have before demonstrated that these articles cannot be increased, but by drawing off more of the labour of the poor from producing the necessaries of life, and such things as they themselves use. Whatever, therefore, the increase of revenue may be from this source, it must bear an exact proportion to the decrease of the necessaries of life, and of the sustenance of the poor.

With respect to the other cause of an increased revenue, viz. the increased taxes, it is in exact proportion to the increased ingenuity, and the more successful invention, of the financier; by which more is drawn from the people in general*; and a still further shortening of the meals of the poor is occasioned. To these two causes the increase of revenues is to be attributed. The effecting of which is too often considered as the greatest achievement of the greatest statesmen. From this they expect

> Egregiam pariter laudem, et spolia ampla referre.
>
> VIRGIL.

We have heard much said of the inexhaustible resources of many civilized powers. That which is meant by these resources is, I apprehend, that the revenues equal the expenses, and that they are capable of increase so as to keep pace with them.

The resources of a nation can be said to increase only when the revenue is capable of increase. The revenue of a

* Vide Section on Taxes.

nation

nation can be capable of increase only by the people's becoming more capable of paying the taxes which compose the revenue. The people who pay all the taxes are either of the class of the rich, or of the class of the poor. The rich can only become able to pay more taxes, by becoming more rich; but they cannot become more rich, except by their claim of the labour of the poor becoming greater, and, of consequence, making the poor still poorer, that is, compellable to render more of their labour to the rich, and of course enjoying fewer of the fruits of it themselves.

The ability of the poor to add to the revenue can only be increased by their increasing in number. The increase of the number of the people is much too slow to keep pace with the increase of the taxes, and is not in such a degree as materially to increase the revenue... The people in no state of Europe have ever increased above the five hundredth part, annually. Whatever fresh taxes are laid on the poor, as will be seen hereafter, are, in effect, laid on the necessaries

of

of life. In both cases, therefore, the increase of the revenue can be effected only by a proportionable decrease of the necessaries of life to the poor*.

There is only one instance which can be an exception to the observation, that all new taxes bear on the poor; namely, where the increased taxes are laid on the rich only, and where they pay them by diminishing their former expense or consumption. In this case, there would be a mere change in the articles consumed, not an increase of the consumption... How often this might be the case cannot be determined. Every man who did not before spend the whole of his income, would now, probably, pay the additional taxes out of his surplus income, and continue spending, i.e. consuming, in the same degree as before. And, wherever it was possible, every person, who spent his

* Nor does the ease with which large loans are obtained show any thing else than the extreme inequality of property subsisting: or, in other words, the magnitude of the power of the rich over the labour of the poor: by which they can force from them such vast quantities of the produce of their labour. But this must end in the extreme exhaustion and misery of the labouring people.

whole

whole income, would endeavour to increase his income, rather than diminish his enjoyments: the landlord would raise his rent, the professional man his fees, and the tradesman the profits of his trade. In all these cases, the private consumption remaining the same, the public consumption is augmented as much as the new taxes amount to; of course, more of the fruits of the labour of the poor is consumed, and the quantity left for them to consume is lessened. Hence the increase of the resources of a nation; or, what is the same thing, the increased revenue is the lessening of the necessaries of life, to the poor, very nearly in proportion to the augmentation of the revenue.

An increase of revenue thus operating as a decrease of the sustenance of man, must have an effect on the number of the people. Where the people, with respect to number, are stationary, it must occasion a decrease; where they are in a state of decrease, it must accelerate it. Hence, therefore, an increase of revenue must have an opposite effect on the number

of

of the people; and, what perhaps is more to be lamented, it must occasion a great augmentation of their misery—by which their decrease of number is ever attended. To suppose always that a people can bear an increase of imposition, which is meant by the term resources, because it is submitted to; and that no visible effect follows from it; is to draw a doubtful conclusion. The complaints of the poor are made with a voice that seldom reaches the Treasuries; and the effect on their numbers will not be known without a more minute inquiry than is usually made.

If taxes increase, and individual wealth also increases, both which are an increased demand on the produce of the labour of the poor, the state of the poor will soon be reduced to one similar to that in China: but whether that degree of want and misery will be born by the nations of northern climates, that is submitted to by the inhabitants of the southern latitudes, the effects of which are to relax their bodies and weaken their minds, may very well be dreaded.

The

The principle that ought universally to guide lawgivers, in imposing taxes, is, that they should bear no harder on one order of people than on another.

---

## SECTION XXVIII.

### ON TAXES.

Taxes are laid both on the superfluities and necessaries of life.

Taxes laid on the superfluities affect the rich only. Taxes on the necessaries of life affect both rich and poor; but they affect them in a different manner. On the rich, both operate as taxes on superfluities; for a rich man will never deprive himself of any necessary of life, whatever additional price a tax may lay on it; he will first part with some superfluity, to pay the tax with: with respect, therefore, to the rich man, all taxes are to be regarded as on superfluities. To the poor man, a tax on the necessaries of life proves really such; and he can no way pay

pay it, but by diminishing the quantity he uses of something necessary to his existence. The deprivation of a necessary of life, and that of a superfluity, are of so different a nature, that no comparison can be made between them; and therefore no difference in the proportion, as to the quantum, can make a tax on the rich and the poor man equal. We have said before, that every tax that is laid on the poor man is, in effect, a tax on the necessaries of life. He uses nothing but what may be strictly looked on as a necessary of life; if he uses any thing that seems to be a superfluity, he must give up some necessary to obtain it. Tea, and tobacco may be thought superfluities; but the state of his stomach requires them: he cannot quiet the cravings of hunger so cheap, or at all, in any other way. That which removes the cravings of hunger, will be allowed to be necessary.

As there can be no comparison between a tax on a superfluity, and a tax on a necessary of life, and as there can be no tax on a necessary, with regard to the rich man, it is rendered impossible to proportion

proportion a tax betwixt a rich man and a poor man. The most just mode of taxation therefore is to tax superfluities only: or, which is the same thing, to tax none but the rich; and those in proportion to their riches.

There is a considerable difficulty in determining the point at which we may suppose riches to commence. We have said, that if every person was allowed to enjoy the whole fruits of his labour, he would enjoy as much of the necessaries of life as a family of the present times, in most countries, which has an income of about one hundred and fifty pounds per annum. We will consider this, therefore, as a state of sufficiency, and this is the state above which, for want of a more definite point, we think all should be obliged to contribute to the expenses of government.

The next matter to be adjusted is the proportion that men of different degrees of riches should pay to the support of government, i. e. be taxed. The common ratio proposed, as I apprehend, is, that if one man has one hundred a year, and another a thousand, the latter should pay

ten

ten times more than the former. This difference is not great enough, as it seems, for this reason: All the things which are used by man, we divide into two kinds, viz. necessaries, and superfluities. It is evident that there is no line to be drawn, on one side of which the things are all absolutely necessary; on the other absolutely superfluous: there is, therefore, an impropriety in using the words necessary and superfluous, for these words do not admit of degree; we will therefore drop them, and substitute the word usefulness in the place of them. We may consider all things used by man as useful, but differing in the degree of usefulness; as in the instance of a pound of bread a day, to the wearing of a diamond of the value of half a million of money. They differ in the degree of usefulness as much as animals do in size; as an elephant does from an insect which requires to be magnified many hundred times, before it is visible *. It should seem that all articles,

* We may therefore suppose a scale to be formed, in the different degrees of which all the articles used by men may be ranged; beginning from those that are necessary to their existence, and rising to those that are utterly superfluous.

in proportion as they are more distant from those that are necessary to support life, would give the least trouble to the owners of them, when parted with; they ought, therefore, first to be taxed: but to determine which those articles are, and in what degree of our scale they rank, may not be readily done. It seems likely that the larger a man's fortune is, the more he has and uses of them, and particularly of those in the upper part of the scale; the diminishing therefore of his fortune is in effect to cut off the least useful or superfluous articles—This is done by laying taxes on income. So far seems clear. But the manner of proportioning the share that men of different degrees of riches ought to bear, of the taxes, is not so evident. Whatever a person of about one hundred and fifty pounds a year uses, are those articles that may be deemed as near the lower extremity of the scale of usefulness, as not to be parted with without much inconvenience. Those things the man of fifty thousand a year uses, are most of them useful only in a very light degree; or they may be called superfluous:

ous: a great number of those ought to be given up for one of those at the lower extreme: but the exact number of these, and from what part of the scale of usefulness these ought to be taken, cannot be precisely determined. But we can readily determine that the present mode is not justly proportioned. We have observed that the present mode is---if a person of one hundred pounds a year pays ten pounds, a man of one thousand pays one hundred pounds a year. In this case the former gives up something highly useful if not necessary to his family, whilst the latter gives up nothing but what is in a much less degree useful, and bordering on such as are superfluous. What a man of ten thousand a year gives up is in a still less degree useful, and approaching still nearer to what is superfluous. It would be desirable that the part each rich man should pay towards the taxes should be regulated by some gradually increasing series; to increase, for instance, as the squares of the income of each person, or in some arithmetic or geometric proportion; this would entirely prevent any arbitrary and partial assump-

assumptions, as is the case at present, where it is evidently in favour of the rich, and that in a greater ratio as they are more rich.

This increasing series, viz. as the squares of the income, seems a very just proportion, till it arises to above 1000*l.* per ann. A proportion similar to this might, no doubt, be applied to larger incomes.

In such a case, a tax would be no grievance. In the first place, it would lessen the real comforts of no one of the taxed persons; in the next place, it would not affect the poor, as it would not increase the consumption: of course it would not call off more than before of the labour of the poor from working in the production of the necessaries of life, and consequently for themselves. Thus we will suppose those rich men spent their incomes before they were taxed, that is, that they consumed to the full amount of them: we will also suppose that the part of their income, taken from them by the tax, is laid out in articles to be consumed by an army or navy in time of war; this would be only changing the articles consumed, not increasing them.

them. Whereas, if you tax the poor, i. e. necessaries, the rich consuming nearly as before, the poor must continue the consumption nearly as before, since that admits of little reduction: of course general consumption is increased by so much as the tax amounts to.

Neither would it in any degree lessen the state and grandeur of the great; for this is merely comparative; and as all would sink together, the fall bearing an exact proportion to the height from which each person falls, the same distance would be kept between them as before. The simile of Bishop Watson (in a pamphlet published some years since) would be perfectly just, when applied to them; but when applied as his Lordship has done it, to all people in general, rich as well as poor, it is not so: for in that case, the poor must give up the necessaries of life, the rich the superfluities—which affect the persons, from whom they are taken, in a very different manner.

## SECTION XXIX.

### RECAPITULATION.

HAVING given, under different heads, the effects of civilization on the mass of the people in most European states; it may not be amiss to draw the most material of them more closely together, so as to bring them under one view.

We have seen that a small number of people in these states have first got possession of the land, the stock on it, and every thing that it produces; and then, by the means of these, have obtained the command of the labour of the people.

This comparatively small part of the people being thus in possession of those things, and the power connected with them, are naturally desirous of securing those their great advantages over the rest of the people; and to put it out of the reach of those people to recover them.

The power they are in the possession of furnishes them with the means of securing itself,

itself, as well as the wealth which is the foundation of it. To avail themselves of this power, the first step is to take the right of making laws, exclusively of the people, but which shall bind the whole people into their own hands, i. e. to assume the legislative power. This they do by means of their wealth.

Having gained this inportant point, the next step was to make use of, and exercise this legislative power, by enacting such laws as would effectually secure to them the objects in view, i. e. to enact laws to secure property. The things of which the people are destitute, namely, the land and its produce, being such things as are in a high degree necessary to the comfort and very existence of the people—to enable the rich to retain these, must require strong and severe laws. This we find was done. The laws securing property in most civilized nations are of the most severe kind; severe in the penalties and punishments inflicted; severe in their long duration; severe by their pain and torture; horrid by the terrors and agonies by which the minds of the

the unhappy sufferers are agitated and distracted, for many months, under their dreadful sentences*.

These few, i. e. the aristocracy, being possessed of the property of the whole people, and having power of claiming almost the whole labour of them; and having also, by the means above mentioned, secured it firmly to themselves; their next consideration is to make use of and apply this labour in such a manner as that it shall produce such things as will most gratify their desires and inclinations, and administer to their ease and pleasure. This is done by the manufactures of various kinds†. These therefore are introduced, and forced on the people by all the means that artifice and power can furnish;

* By the laws of England, there are above 160 different offences which subject the parties, when found guilty, to death without benefit of clergy.

From the year 1792, to 1799 inclusive, were discharged from goals and hulks, in London, 21,893 persons.—P. Colquhoun, L L. D.

† There are many persons, no doubt, who really think that the manufactures benefit the people, and act with sincerity in promoting them; but there are many others who cannot be ignorant of their effects.

notwith-

notwithstanding the employments are such as include every thing that human nature, till by long habit it is broke to it, feels irksome, nauseous, painful: and notwithstanding they are unwholesome, debasing, and destructive of mind and body, to such employments nineteen-twentieths of the men, their wives and infants, are condemned, during all the years, months, and days of their lives; enjoying a very small part of what their labour yields. These employments, together with their poverty and want, occasion the miseries and mortality before stated.

Most of the civilized states of Europe, not content with bringing miseries on their own people, extend their baneful influence to nations, inhabitants of the remotest parts of the earth. How many millions of the most harmless and innocent race of people to be found, have been by a few avaricious traders reduced to misery and famine! How many from Africa have been brought to a worse condition than our cattle, by other sets of traders!

The sum therefore of the effects of civilization, in most civilized states, is to enable

enable a few of mankind to attain all possible enjoyments both of mind and body, that their nature is susceptible of; but at the expense, and by depriving the bulk of mankind of the necessaries and comforts of life, by which a great proportion of them is destroyed, and the remainder reduced both corporally and mentally far below the most savage and barbarous state of man. All these things being brought about in a regular, orderly, silent manner; under specious forms, with the external appearance of liberty, and even of charity; greater deprivations are submitted to by the poor, and more oppression exercised over them, by this cool, deliberate, systematic junction of art and force, than force alone was ever known to accomplish.

This, as we have said, is the actual state of things in most civilized countries: but I by no means assert that this state was brought about by the express design or the contrivance of any set of people in these communities. After the assumption of the land in large parcels, and the inequality of other property, which was the

conse-

consequence of it, took place; it is probable that the power which followed, in those that possessed that property, over the rest of the people, was the spontaneous and almost necessary cause of the present system, in most civilized states: but we are not, on that account, to be less anxious for its amendment.

---

## SECTION XXX.

### THE METHOD PROPOSED FOR THE REMOVAL OF THE EVILS COMPLAINED OF.

HAVING now stated the unhappy situation of the mass of the people in most civilized nations, and also assigned what I apprehend to be the true cause of it; it now remains to propose a remedy for it: but

*Hoc opus, hic labor.*

This

This however does not arise from any difficulty in finding an appropriate remedy; for when the true cause of a disease is discovered, we are seldom at a loss for a cure. The difficulty arises from the unwillingness of those who occasion the evil, and who imagine that it is for their interest that it should continue, to permit the remedy to be applied.

An antient physician says, that all changes in the constitution, though even from worse to better, ought to be gradual. I believe the same caution will still be more necessary in regard to the political constitution: great disorder and even convulsions are apt to be raised in both constitutions, by a hasty and indiscreet use of powerful remedies. But it has been found by experience that the human constitution will bear, in large quantities, powerful medicines, if administered with skill and caution. The remedy I have to propose in the disease of civilized society is powerful, and a powerful one in this case seems to be required. It is not, however, a dangerous one, and may be safely committed to the hands of such

persons

persons as are disinterested and dispassionate. To obtain such persons, they should be taken not from the aggrieved party; for from that quarter they would not probably be cool and temperate: their feelings, from the pressure which they have undergone, would probably urge them on too violently. On the contrary, as neutral persons are hard to be found, they should be taken from the *aggrievers*, or the aggrieving party; for, though we may be inclined to do justice, we are seldom so hasty and violent in doing it to others, as we are to have it done to ourselves. Such persons might be safely entrusted with the management of the most powerful means. It would be better therefore that the redress of the grievances of the poor should originate from the rich themselves.

The cause of the evil having been demonstrated to be the great inequality of wealth, the remedy must necessarily be, either to remove this inequality, or to counteract and to prevent its effects. As to the first, I would only propose the abolition of the law of primogeniture, which

which is to be found in most nations, and the annulling of which, in the course of no long time, would, as has been before shown, have greater effects than may be imagined. It is a practice which, to consider it in a private view, does not seem conducive to the happiness of the people; a practice that makes beggars frequently of all the children but one; and, if the parent has an equal affection for all of them, is scarcely a less grievance to him than to the younger children. A possessor of a large estate has in this case but one, perhaps, of a large family provided for; and to provide for the others in a way in any degree suitable to the manner in which he has brought them up, or that would be expected from him, he is embarrassed all his life—and not one father in twenty has the conduct to effect it. A law attended with these circumstances would not, as it should seem, have been continued so long, had there not been some reason, not avowed, for it. A family with a head raised so much above the rest gives a miniature of monarchy, and has from that resemblance, and from other

reasons,

reasons, been supposed inclinable to support prerogative. Alas! how few institutions in most states have the good of the public in view, either in their origin or continuance!

As to the other mode; namely, to prevent the effects of wealth. It has been shown that the chief effect of the unequal distribution of property is the drawing off the labour of the poor from producing the necessaries of life, and employing it in producing the refined manufactures. The obvious remedy, therefore, is the prohibition, by law, of these refined manufactures, or the subjecting them to such heavy taxes as would much lessen the production of them. The direct operation of this would be the prevention of the effects of the alleged cause: this would be drawing the venom from the jaws of the serpent, and depriving him of the power of destruction: this would prove an effectual cure, and that in a manner safe, peaceable, and constitutional; liable to occasion no disorder in the constitution, no convulsion in the state; and requires nothing to be put in execution, but

a real

a real desire in the rich of redressing the grievances of the poor. Neither is it a novel, untried method; the enacting sumptuary laws having been the practice in many states and ages. Here, then, is the cure, not Utopian, but simple in its nature, easy in practice, and certain in effect.

The advantages of this method are obvious. In the first place, the change may be introduced by as slow degrees as shall be found requisite; so as not to throw artificers out of employ, till labour is found for them in agriculture, and the arts subservient to it; which will soon be the case, as the capitals before employed in the refined manufactures, now less in demand, will of course be transferred to agriculture, &c.*

Another circumstance that renders this mode less exceptionable is, that it will alleviate the miseries, and bring comforts to the poor, without in any proportion diminishing the gratification of the rich man, Will the latter be less warm in a

* See Note P.

second cloth than he was in a superfine? Will he sit easier in a carved than a plain chair? Will he sleep better in a silk than in a linen bed? Will he eat less heartily, his appetite unhurt by excesses, on plain beef and mutton, than he now does on high-seasoned dishes, unnaturally provoking it? The truth is, the pleasures which the rich enjoy are by no means equal to the sufferings the poor undergo, in the present system.

It has been observed, that in every science, the more thoroughly it is understood, the fewer and more simple are its principles and precepts: hence the remedy proposed, being single, and in its nature simple, carries a presumption with it that the true case of the evil in question has been assigned.

## SECTION XXXI.

### OBJECTIONS ANSWERED.

If the facts produced in the foregoing treatise, and the reasonings founded on them, be true and just, it is evident that the far greater part of the labour and industry of mankind is ill directed; and, instead of being beneficial, is highly prejudicial to them. The subject of it, therefore, is of the greatest importance to the civilized world: no other subject affects so great a number of men, nor so nearly, as this does. Hence, therefore, it seems that no apology should be required from any person who should endeavour to throw a light on it. But there will probably be, notwithstanding, some persons whose blame will be incurred by an attempt of this kind. They may say that such inquiries have a strong tendency to render the poor discontented.

In

In answer to this it might be said, that a representation of the hardships and sufferings of the poor will have very little effect in occasioning the discontent apprehended, if those sufferings and hardships are not real. If the poor do not undergo and feel those disadvantages, neither what has been said here, nor what can possibly be said, will make them believe they do, and consequently cannot create discontent. Is such an apprehension, therefore, to suppress all inquiries in this matter, and to prevent all endeavours to draw the attention of the public towards it? But if their grievances are real, who is the man that will say that these, and the causes of them, ought not to be made public? Are almost the whole of mankind to remain objects of oppression and injustice, without any hopes of, or any means taken to obtain an alleviation of their sufferings and degraded state, forever?

But, if it is allowed that the evils of the poor are to be regarded, and that means are to be used for their relief, what

what other method can be had recourse to, than that of inquiring into the reality of the existence of those evils, and discovering the cause of them? If this is not done, how can the aggrieved apply for redress; or the *aggrievers*, though inclined to do it, grant the redress required?

If any man thinks the people suffer the calamities which I have declared myself to believe they do; and also if he is persuaded that the cause assigned is the true cause of these calamities; if he thinks this is not at all, or not sufficiently known; can he, if the principles of justice, humanity, true patriotism, or religion, have any influence on his mind, do otherwise than I have done?

These sufferings of the poor, in order to be seen, it has not been necessary to go in search of them; they occur every where, and obtrude themselves on every body's notice: more frequently, no doubt, more unavoidably and affectingly, to a medical practitioner than to any other person. A physician does not go out of his way; does not officiously make in-

quiries

quiries in a subject he has no concern with; does not deviate from his proper line of duty, which is to alleviate, by all means in his power, the sufferings of man; does not intrude his opinion on matters he has no knowledge of, nor presume to judge of that which he has not received the proper means of enabling him to form a judgment of.

I trust, therefore, it will appear to every humane and candid mind,

1st, That the direct intention of this work is to discover a remedy for the evils attending civilization.

2dly, That, in order to discover and make known this remedy, it was necessary to inquire into and discover the cause of the evils.

3dly, That, in order to discover and demonstrate the cause of the evils, it was necessary to investigate their nature, and the reality of their existence.

4thly, That, in order to induce those who had it in their power to remove those evils, and administer relief to the sufferers, it was necessary to state them in a full manner, and to demonstrate the cause of them;

them; and that especially because those persons who are the causes of them, are probably ignorant of their being so.

If therefore the direct and obvious intention of the book is as above, and the means used to obtain what is intended are natural and necessary, the author cannot be responsible, or in any degree blamable, for the oblique applications and consequences that may be apprehended from his statement of the evils, or of the inquiry into the cause of them.

The apprehensions that are entertained, are, that the people, from the foregoing statements, may possibly be more sensible of the hardships they suffer, and therefore bear them less patiently; and that, being made acquainted with the cause of them, might be induced to use endeavours to remove them. With respect to the former objection, it has been already answered; with respect to the latter, namely, the discovering the cause of their sufferings, if the cause is the true one, I hope there will not be found one man in Europe who will not be ashamed to say that it ought not to be discovered.

If

If the cause assigned be not the true cause, it ought by reason and argument to be shown that it is not the true cause; as by such discussion only the true one can ever be expected to be dicovered. Are we rather to admit a present and greater evil, than one that is less, and in apprehension only?

In fine, it is to be considered that the subject of this work does not relate to a few persons, to a small portion of mankind; that it does not relate to some inconsiderable inconveniences only, which may attend them; but that it concerns the great mass of the people, the bulk of mankind, the inhabitants of the land, as far as civilized nations, or the power of civilized nations, that is, to almost all the known world, extends: and that the object of it is to remove the greatest evils that can afflict all this great part of mankind—their hunger, their nakedness, their disease, and premature death.

## SECTION XXXII.

### THE CAUSE OF THE DIFFERENT OPINIONS ON THIS SUBJECT.

It must be owing to some particular cause, that opinions so distant from the truth are so generally held.

This is, evidently, because the subject is not open to fair, and unbiassed discussion, like other branches of knowledge. It is somewhat complex and abstract, and therefore can be treated only by people of education. But, unfortunately for the poor, few of these are to be found in their order; and still fewer who will take up their cause, contrary to their own interest. Persons of education are generally of some property, of the learned professions, or privileged orders; for whose interest it is that things should remain as they are. So far, therefore, are they

they from investigating the matter with disinterestedness, and a real desire of discovering the truth, that they with great industry discountenance and oppose such inquiries being made by other people, and endeavour to render such truly philanthropic attempts unpopular and uncreditable; branding such people with the odious names of innovators, levellers, &c. Hence, the state of our knowledge and practice on this subject, by far the most important to the human race, is as it was several centuries ago, and in times of the greatest ignorance and darkness.

SEC-

## SECTION XXXIII.

### THAT THE FACTS SET FORTH IN THIS WORK, AND THE CAUSES OF THEM, ARE NOT GENERALLY KNOWN.

FROM every information which I have received, both from such writers as have fallen into my hands, and from general conversation, I have reason to think that the principal facts set forth in this work are not at all, or but little known; insomuch, that it might be considered as a phenomenon in the civilized world, not a little extraordinary. I think, however, that it may be accounted for, in some degree at least, in this manner, viz. by considering that those persons, whether authors or others, that were most likely to discover truths of this kind, are people who do not expect to be benefited by the discovery of them. I do not say this as reflecting on mankind, by insinuating that

that they were wilfully blind to the knowledge of the above facts; but we well know that few discoveries are made, in any of the arts, in which the inventors of them are not interested. Necessity, that is, the highest degree of interest, is the parent of invention; and we may say, the only parent who produces it. Men can very rarely employ their thoughts intensely on any subject which is of no concern to them. On the other hand, in case our interest is against any discovery, if any thoughts arise in the mind concerning it, they are unattended to, or are soon suppressed, as useless or disadvantageous; and this often passes in the minds of people unobserved, and without their being conscious of this their seemingly unfair and uncandid mode of proceeding. As our interest secretly biasses us in favour of every thing that promotes itself, so does it secretly divert us from every thing that opposes itself.

Whether this accounts satisfactorily for the phenomenon or not, I will not say, but it is difficult to ascribe it to any other cause that is more probable. It is certain

certain that most of the facts stated, and the observations on them, are not known; or, if known by some certain persons, are intentionally suppressed, and kept back from the knowledge of the public. Is it generally known by the rich, that there is great reason to think that, out of nine or ten millions of people, no less a number than five hundred thousand die annually for want? That the poor do not enjoy that content of mind which they are usually represented to do? Are they (the rich) aware of the pernicious effects of wealth, and the manner in which it operates in the production of these effects? Are they sensible of the real tendency of manufactures, trade, and commerce—that they retract from millions the necessaries of life? Are they not, on the contrary, taught to believe, that, by encouraging them, they benefit the poor? Are they aware that they themselves are the real efficient causes of all the miseries of the poor; assured, as they have ever been, that they were the source of all the plenty and comforts of the poor? Are they sensible that the

situation

situation of the poor is not necessarily such as it is—but that it is the direct and necessary consequence of the system of civilization? Are they sensible that the effects of civilization, with regard to a nation, considered as the collected body of the people, are contrary to what they are commonly supposed to be, viz. to weaken a nation, to impoverish a nation, to render a people more ignorant and more barbarous? Are they, the rich, sensible that they take to themselves, without moving one of their fingers in producing them, nine-tenths of the products of all the labour of the poor; and only leave them the remaining one-tenth to subsist on? Do the rich consider that every thing they use or consume, though apparently so different from the coarse food, coarse clothing, &c. of the poor; for instance, when they are wearing their fine laces, their silver and gold silks, their diamonds, &c.; when they are sitting in their costly carriages; in short, in almost every action of their lives—that they are wasting and consuming the bread, the clothing, and the fuel, of the poor?

poor? Is all this commonly known to the rich? If it is not, ought it not to be made known to them; to them who are the causes of it; to them who have it in their power to remove and remedy it; to them, of whom many, no doubt, when they know it, will be instantly disposed to apply the proper means to cure it? Are not such, therefore, to be made acquainted with the effects of their own actions—or is it a principle, and a determined resolution, in most civilized states, that the representations of the grievances of the poor, and the demonstration of the causes of them, however great the former, or however clear the latter, are never to be made public, lest the poor should get a knowledge of them? I have presumed that this is not the case, but that when the rulers in most civilized states, and the wealthy subjects of them, are informed of the evils they perhaps unknowingly occasion, they will consent to such means as are necessary to remove them: and this has been the motive and expectation that has produced the present work.

## SECTION XXXIV.

### ON THE MEANS OF LESSENING A SCARCITY, WHEN EXISTING.

We have shown that the prevention of a scarcity of the necessaries of life can only be effected by removing the cause, which, as we have shown also, is the employing too few hands in agriculture. But this preventive method can only take place at some distance of time prior to the existence of the scarcity. When this actually presses, other methods must be had recourse to.

On the occasion of the late scarce seasons, (I am now speaking with respect to England) several methods were taken, and many more proposed, which were not put in execution. Some of these means were really intended, and were well adapted, to lessen the evil. Others were designed rather to amuse and silence the complaints of the people, than to afford any

any great relief. Of the latter kind, were the calumnies and prosecutions against the millers, regraters, &c. and the methods made use of to force the farmers to bring their corn to market. To these may be added the serving out corn at reduced prices. We shall presently see that these methods were both ineffectual and bearing unequally.

The former methods, namely, those that would have the effect of lessening the scarcity and preventing the famine, could only be of two kinds, viz. the increasing the quantity of provisions in the land; and the more frugal use of those already in it. The former of these is to be done only by importation. With respect to the latter, various methods may be taken. That retrenchment could only take place in the consumption of the rich, is evident. The poor were sufficiently stinted by the high price provisions sold at. It might be asked, what were the articles in which the rich abridged themselves? None, I believe, were thought of but that of bread. Bread, it was said, was the staff of life—it was therefore thought sufficient to be sparing

in

in the use of that. In the consumption of other kinds of food, they gave themselves the same latitude as before. There were very few even that pretended to do more. But it should be considered that the mass of food, or that which is the sustenance of man, consists of articles of various sorts; and whatever is wasted, of any one kind, lessens the quantity of the whole; and, of course, the whole quantum or aggregate of the sustenance of man: and there are very few articles which the rich use, that would not be more proper to abridge themselves in the use of than bread. Bread is much less nutritious than most other substances which we use as food; such as beef, mutton, pork, venison, fish, cheese, butter, &c. A retrenchment in any of these articles would have been of more service to the poor than in that of bread; and in most of which there might have been a much greater saving: for of bread, little is used among the luxurious or their servants; of course, little can be saved from it. This, I fear, the rich made choice of, not because it was the most proper article, but because it was the least sacrifice, and required the least self-denial. A few ounces only of bread are eaten at a meal by the luxurious; but in their soups, their gravies, their sauces, their stews, &c. a very large quantity of animal food is consumed; an ounce of which affords more nourishment to a poor man, and better supports him under his labour, than three times the quantity of bread, or of almost any kind of vegetable. We will put the gratifying of the appetites of the poor, though there is no reason why that should be done, out of the question. A great deal of barley, which would have been of great use, in that extremity, for bread, might have been saved, by lessening the profuse use of ale amongst the servants and retainers of the rich. But a still greater saving might have been made by the rich, if they had withdrawn the quantity of oats that were given to their carriage horses, their hunters, their race, saddle, and army horses; but this, though pointed out, was not put in practice: this would have reduced the condition and high order of their horses; and to have

seen

seen the horses in that state, would have given more pain than it did to see the thin, pale, squallid faces of the poor. If the humanity of the rich had reached to this mode of relieving the poor, it would have done a great deal more than all the other means did, that were made use of *.

The retrenchment, however, in the use of any of the articles of food, certainly as far as it went, was a real alleviation of the distresses of the poor; but it did not, alas! go far.

The other methods that were chiefly used had not, I am afraid, this effect. These were the subscriptions that were set on foot, to give the poor corn, &c. or to sell it them at reduced prices: and, what was chiefly relied on, the obliging the parish officers in England to serve out to the poor certain quantities of corn,

* The raising the provender for horses takes up a great part of the land. In the open parts of the kingdom, which till lately contained a great share of it, beans were grown alternately with wheat; so that they occupied nearly one-half of the land. They were almost wholly used for horses. From this circumstance it appears, how great a part of the land in those parts is employed to raise provender. It is no doubt the same in other countries, though there it is not so evident.—The hay is not taken into this account.

weekly; which was not confined to the paupers, but all the labouring people of the parish were furnished with it. These were the proceedings alluded to as ineffectual*. The latter was very heavy, amounting to infinitely more than all the other contributions, and was very grievous to the farmers, having doubled and even trebled their before high poor-rates. It is just that the rich should contribute to the poor according, and in proportion to their ability: but a farmer, if we estimate it either as to the capital he is master of and employs in his business, or as, to his income, contributes ten times as much to the poor as the draper, who is only rated according to the rent of the house he lives in. To make this appear, we will suppose the farmer to rent 200*l.* per annum, and that the produce of the farm is three times the rent, i. e. 600*l.*; one-third of this goes to the landlord, another for labour, and a third to the farmer, to support himself and family. The farmer is rated at 200*l.* but the draper, whose

* Vide, p. 234,

income

income also may be 200*l.* per annum, is rated only at 20*l.* perhaps, for his house, i. e. one-tenth of what the farmer is. It is true the stock in trade of the draper is liable, in this country, to be rated to the poor; but the law is so tender, lest the tradesman's credit should be hurt by too nice an examination into the value of his stock, that the fact is, he is scarcely ever assessed for his stock; and when he is, it is always greatly under its amount. It might be said that the farmer is allowed for his poor-rates in his rent: be this as it may, this additional burden by a new express law, and particularly bearing on them, was never expected, and of course could never be allowed for. Freeholders, occupying their own small estates, certainly felt the whole weight of it.

The farmer, next the labourer, is infinitely the greatest benefactor to his fellow creatures; yet he is, notwithstanding, a very unpopular character, in most states. This his unpopularity is brought about, as we have seen before, by the mercenary means made use of, by which the opinion is sedulously propagated among the poor.

The

The owners of the land, though their whole employment is to consume, without moving a finger towards the reproducing of that which they consume, are considered in a much less invidious light than the farmers, the greatest number of whom work hard in raising the necessaries of life, and partake very sparingly in the use of them*.

But, as we have said before, the method above mentioned, made use of to relieve the poor, was not only ineffectual as to the end in view; but tending greatly to increase the evil. In a scarcity, the quantity of corn the season produces is insufficient to supply the people until the next harvest. In this case, it ought to be so managed, and served out to the people in such a quantity, as to hold out, without the necessity of diminishing that quantity, till the harvest: in the same same manner as on board a ship at sea, the crew are put upon short allowance. The price of corn (in this term we include all other provisions) being raised according

* Vide Note IV.

to

to the quantity in the country, does the duty of the officer at sea, that serves out the bread, &c. to the crew. The people are limited in their consumption, by the money they have to lay out in corn, &c. If the price is high, they buy less, so as not to exceed the quantity prescribed as it were by the scarcity. But if money is given to them, by which they can buy more; or if they are furnished with corn at a lower rate than the market price; they will consume daily in such quantities, that it would not last till the harvest: so that in the latter end of the summer, there would be no corn in the land, and an absolute famine would be the consequence. The use therefore that the distribution of money could be of, would be then only, when given to very poor people who did not earn the average wages, enabling them, by the assistance of that, to purchase the quantity equal to what the poor in general could buy.

If the knowledge of the quantity of corn in the country could be by any means obtained, as it may on board a vessel,

vessel, the ratio might be proportioned with more exactness; but as we are all convinced that that cannot be done, the best course is to be guided by the price, which is probably always, at least generally, regulated by the quantity of corn there is to be brought to market; if there is no officious interference to prevent its being so, by magistrates, or collections or riots of the people.

---

## SECTION XXXV.

### WHETHER THE CULTIVATION OF COMMONS IN ENGLAND WOULD PREVENT SCARCITY THERE.

It has frequently been proposed, as the means of obtaining a greater plenty of the necessaries of life, to bring into a state of cultivation the moors and commons, of which there are a great quantity dispersed

dispersed in the different parts of the kingdom of England.

In order to judge of the propriety and the tendency of this measure, to produce the end that was had in view, we must consider the nature of the different kinds of commons; as far at least as is necessary to resolve this question; which is of considerable moment to the public, and to the poor in particular of this nation.

All the different kinds of commons cannot be here enumerated, nor is it necessary for the present purpose.

The first kind to be distinguished from others is, those common pieces of land that are found in common and open fields, in the unenclosed parts of the kingdom; viz. Gloucestershire, Oxfordshire, Northamptonshire, Warwickshire, Leicestershire, Lincolnshire, and many others. These parcels of land in the open fields are used as pastures for the milch cows and other cattle; or are sheep-walks, and belonging to the farmers who hold the arable parts, which are in a state of severalty. These, in the open

state

state of the parishes, cannot probably be better applied. After the enclosure takes place, they are generally ploughed up, if the soil is proper for it.

Other commons may be divided into forests, moors, downs, &c. Some of these latter are frequently private property. The only distinction among them, that need be made as to the subject of this inquiry, namely, whether they ought to be broke up or not, is, that they are of two kinds, viz. such as will immediately bear good corn crops with little labour and expense; and others that require great labour and expense, and also time, to bring them about, as it is called.

Of the first sort, there are many commons and downs in the western part of Devonshire, and in Cornwall. Many of these, or parts of these, being pared, burnt, and limed, will with one ploughing bear great and good crops of wheat, and a crop or two of oats (the third crop perhaps is improperly taken); after which they are laid down to pasture, which is generally as good at least as it was before. There is no doubt, therefore, as to the

advantage

advantage of raising crops of grain from them; since, as walks for sheep, or pastures for lean beasts, they yield little profit for the owner or the public.

The second sort is so much the greater in number and quantity, as almost to deserve to be considered as the only commons in the kingdom. These lands require great labour, time, and expense, before they can be brought to bear any tolerable crops of grain, turnips, or grass. And notwithstanding the cultivation of these may answer the proprietor's views, it does not those of the public; for it happens, in this instance, that his interest and that of the public are different: the proprietor's expense is repaid not altogether by the present annual produce; he is creating, as it were, a fee-simple estate, and therefore expects his whole return only at some distance of time: but the public is interested in the quantum of the annual produce; and for it to answer the proposed views, the produce should be immediate. If therefore any considerable number of hands were taken off from the working on other

and

and better lands, and employed on these commons, the consequence would be a great reduction in the quantity of the necessaries of life. The richer the land, the greater the quantity of provisions is yielded by the labour bestowed on it. Until the good land therefore is cultivated in the utmost possible perfection, the labour should not be taken off from it, and applied to the poor lands. It has been demonstrated before that the powers of the land, i. e. the fertility, being given, the produce is in proportion to the labour bestowed upon it. The converse of the proposition is, that the quantity of labour being given, the produce is in proportion to the goodness of the land. The present remedy therefore, as has been shown, and which will be the proper remedy for many years to come, is to put more hands to work on the land that is already in a state of cultivation.

## SECTION XXXVI.

### ON THE RISING ARISTOCRACY OF THE AMERICAN STATES.

It has been before observed that there is a very striking difference between these states and any of the European nations; we except some of the remote parts of the Russian empire, as the condition of them is little known; and in that circumstance which chiefly distinguishes the European from the American states, the contrast is not so strong.

This difference consists in the greater increase of the people in the American states, they doubling every fifteen or twenty years. Those in Europe do not double in five hundred.

This greater increase of the people of America cannot be attributed to the climate; that of few or probably of none of these states being so favourable to the health of mankind as the European; and

and three or four of the states are justly considered as unhealthy, being, from the excessive heat, putrid marshes, and overflowing rivers, subject to very destructive fevers: the increase therefore is not to be looked for from that, or, probably, any other physical cause.

It is, no doubt, owing to the cause which we have before suggested, namely, their inhabitants being better sustained; and this arises from the whole land not being appropriated in the manner that it is in Europe; on which account the poor can easily, at least more easily, obtain sufficient means, with their industry, to rear up the children that are born: which we have seen is not the case in Europe. Their employments, which are almost wholly in the fields, being of a much more wholesome nature than that of manufacturers, are another cause contributing to the rapid increase of the people.

Notwithstanding this circumstance, which is not only an indication of the superiority of their condition, but itself constitutes

constitutes that superiority ; and, notwithstanding its present state is in most other respects so much more advantageous than that of Europe ; yet it is observable how earnest and impatient the people in America are to arrive at a similar situation to that of the nations of Europe ; and, in consequence of this, what endeavours are making to obtain it. As the measures now taking may have a different operation from what is expected, it behoves them well to consider the matter, before they go so far in the business that it will be too late for them to recede. Their situation at present is evidently thriving. Is any material change therefore advisable ?

The Americans, it cannot be doubted, have a knowledge of the peculiarities of their own situation : and it seems to me that they might acquire a just idea of that of the European states, by considering some of the facts stated in this treatise; and by that means be enabled to make the comparison between them, and form a judgment whether any change be necessary to be made in their own state, and what practices of the European states are to be avoided by themselves.

One leading object with the American states seems to be the increase of the people. They may be induced to wish this, partly from a fallacious principle. They think that by an augmentation of their number, they shall be better enabled to defend themselves against any attempts of the European powers to subjugate them. This idea is just: it is however, perhaps, unnecessary to be acted on; from the consideration of their remote situation, and the failure of an attempt of that kind by one of the most powerful of them; and of their being now so much stronger than they were at the time of that contest. The other idea, and which we think fallacious, is, that the riches of a country consist in the number of its inhabitants. Concerning this, we have before spoken.

But admitting both those advantages which are expected from the increased number of the people, do they take the

right

right course to obtain it? to wit, by the introduction of manufactures, which they have endeavoured hitherto, *invitâ Minervâ*, to establish among themselves. On this subject they think with the many—that manufactures will give them a balance of trade, and consequently enrich; and that they will increase the number of the people. It is not necessary to repeat the refutation of these opinions.

At present, the Americans enjoy many of the advantages of an equal state of property; but it is not because there are not in America a considerable number of rich men; and that an aristocracy has not considerable footing and weight there; but it is because there is room backwards for the poor to recede from the wealthy, and by these means to get beyond the reach of the lash of their whip: they can back, in the coachman's phrase, till they arrive at places where they can work for themselves, and receive all the fruits of their labour, which cannot be done where the land is engrossed by the few. But this state will not probably last many ages:

ages: they are taking the most direct methods that can be devised to establish an universal aristocracy.

The state, it is understood, claims the disposal of all the unsettled lands, and is now selling them, and applying the produce in paying off the national debt. This seems, on this last consideration, a just and proper measure; and it is improper only as to the mode in which it is done. The objectionable part of it is, that they grant it in large tracts, consisting of two or three hundred thousand acres or more, to one person; who either keeps it, till, by the settlements coming up to him, the land becomes more valuable, or sells it out to other people still in large parcels of several thousand acres each. Here is at once the foundation of great landed property. These grandees in an age or two will have estates as large as the princes of the blood in France lately had. Here is at once the establishment of allodial lords, or of more modern nobility—dukes, counts, barons, &c. It matters little whether they have these titles or not, they will have all the power

which

which the people of these orders hold in Europe. If manufactures are not introduced, these great proprietors will support their authority by keeping up a large number of retainers, as the ancient barons did. If manufactures are introduced, they will keep up their influence by means of their wealth, as the great proprietors in Europe do in the present times. The labourers and manufacturers, or the vassals and boors, will be just in the same situation as they are in France; or in Germany, Livonia, Estonia, &c.

There is the same division of the people observable in America, that there is in Europe; the inhabitants are divided into rich and poor there also; with this difference, that the rich bear a less proportion in the former than in the latter. The rich in America are composed of people who have large tracts of land granted them, or are become rich by traffic and commerce. But the proportion of little proprietors is much greater than in Europe; and the labourers are both fewer in number, and their condition much nearer that of the small proprietors;

to

to which order they are every day rising. Their wages being high, and provisions cheap, of course their savings soon enable them to become owners of small parcels of land; and the chance of being such, makes them industrious and frugal, which again is a cause of putting it sooner in their power of being so.

This perhaps is the most happy situation to be met with in this present life—affording constant excitements to industry and action, and equally certain rewards to that active industry. We therefore may very justly apply to the Americans the lines in Virgil,

> O fortunatos nimiùm, sua si bona norint,
> Agricolas!

This happy situation of the people will, as it has been remarked before, be of no long continuance. The rich have not only the degree of power that riches give; but by this power they have already gained the additional one of filling the house of representatives, senate, presidency,

sidency, and all the other lucrative and influential situations.

It is to be feared, too, that they will adopt all the same delusive arts, to obtain their own views, which we have observed are made use of in Europe. The people are made to believe that they cannot be a great people but by means of trade, manufactures, and commerce. This is natural: it is natural to gratify our own desires at the expense of others: at least this is so frequently done as to seem natural to man. The rich cannot have the elegant and luxurious enjoyments, without the manufactures; to plant which, therefore, among themselves, is the object in view. But it will be difficult to persuade the people that to be confined to their workshops is more wholesome and pleasant than working in the field; and if persuasion is only relied on, the work will be slow. But the operation of the other measures, viz. the granting the great estates, will soon have its full force, and produce the same effects as it has done in Europe: and as this will

be

be aided by the fortunes already acquired by the merchants, tradesmen, &c. it will be sooner brought about.

It is a childish precaution in the states to refrain from creating any orders of nobility; whilst they are laying the most solid foundation for their future establishment, in granting such large tracts of land to single persons. It is a matter of little consequence whether a *Spencer*, with seventy thousand a year, is called duke of Marlborough or not—is his influence a consequence of having that title, or of having the seventy thousand a year?

The requiring the possession of property, as a qualification for holding places in the senate, house of representatives, &c. in congress, and in the several separate states, is a proof that an aristocracy has already obtained in a considerable degree, and also is the means of augmenting it.

The means most effectual for obtaining the desired population, would be the granting lands in small quantities, gratis, to all such persons as would form settlements on them; and the opposing the introduction of all such manufactures as are not necessary; as are not of the coarser kind; and are not principally subservient to agriculture.

It must happen, in the course of time, that the whole world, and every part of it, will be fully peopled; and that the produce of it will be insufficient for the support of the inhabitants, however well cultivated it might be; but this period must be very remote, and the event cannot be prevented by any human means: we ought not to anticipate the evil by any systems or practices of our own. This, perhaps, may be the term intended by the Creator for it's continuance, it being, as it seems, inconsistent with his benevolence to extend the existence of a habitable world, after it ceases to afford the means of giving happiness to its inhabitants. It were well if the intentions of man were equally benevolent. This is not the only instance in which the designs of Providence are frustrated by

man,

man, and particularly by the *rulers* of man.

## SECTION XXXVII.

### HAPPIEST STATE.

A PEOPLE who, from an extreme civilization, should descend to a medium state, i. e. to one equally distant from their own, and that of a savage, would probably be placed in that situation which would be the happiest that human nature is capable of enjoying. Mr. Hume, after many other writers, placed the happiness of mankind, as we have before observed, and in part discussed, in action, pleasure, and rest, or ease. He is, perhaps, right in the choice he has made of his ingredients; but is, I apprehend, totally wrong in supposing them to be possessed by the people in general of of civilized nations. Some of these advantages are really enjoyed by some in those states, but they are to be found united in a very few only. By some of the individuals, pleasure, and rest, or ease, are exclusively enjoyed: on others, action, but it is laborious action, is imposed. The rich have their rest and their ease to excess; and therefore have little enjoyment in them. The poor have their action or labour also in excess, to the exclusion of their pleasure and their ease; and therefore to their great grievance, and not happiness. What Mr. Hume says is applicable only to the few, if any, in those refined states in which these three ingredients are found in due mixture and proportion: and therefore it was ascribed to civilized people in a manner that, from so accurate a philosopher as Mr. Hume was, would hardly have been expected. Nor is it probable that it is generally enjoyed by any society of people any where existing: not by the civilized people, for the causes we have seen—not by the savage people, from

from their unequal exercise, of hunting, and the uncertainty of its obtaining its end.

This, namely, the proportion and mixture of Mr. Hume's ingredients, is, however, I think, attainable by any civilized state which has the wisdom and justice to submit to the means of obtaining it.

In order to put it in the power of the whole, or the bulk of the people in a nation, to enjoy that proper proportion of action and rest, by the interchange of which the third ingredient spontaneously follows, two means are necessary, viz. 1st, That each man should labour so much only as is necessary for his family; and, 2dly, That he should enjoy the whole fruits of his labour. This would give the proper proportion of action, so as to leave the necessary time for rest, which, by the interchange, would give reciprocally to each other its due relish; of which the third ingredient, pleasure, is chiefly composed. This relish of the action and labour would not be lessened by the apprehension that the end expected from it would not be obtained.

We have seen the quantity of the produce of the poor is eight or ten times greater than the quantity consumed by themselves; consequently, one eighth or tenth part of the time he is now confined to labour would be sufficient to furnish him with those things which he at present enjoys; or if he should, as he would, no doubt, choose to be better supplied, one-fourth, or one-third of the time he is now confined to labour, would be sufficient to obtain plenty for himself and his family: and this would perhaps be rendered less, by retaining such machinery as would be applicable to the coarse manufactures, which would yet be useful in this medium state—thus availing ourselves, for the use and real benefit of the people, of that which has been hitherto applied to uses so injurious to them. Three-fourths or two-thirds of their time the whole people might really enjoy, as Mr. Hume supposes, their pleasure and ease, and would truly substantiate, in this medium state, his assertion, which, in the state he applied it to, was in a great measure false.

To

To men who are not by their intemperance, which in this state of things would be a rare vice, for men are seldom intemperate in the use of such things as they themselves produce by their own labour; I say, to men who are not urged by intemperance to vicious pursuits, their greatest proportion of pleasure would arise from their employing their leisure in study and contemplation, and in the improvement of their minds; whilst for this pleasure their action and relaxation would give them the true taste.

In the present state, the same degree of wealth which gives leisure for application to intellectual exercises, furnishes also the means of luxury and intemperance, and other methods of indulging the passions; and thus calls off the attention from mental improvement. This the medium state would not do, which would be the occasion of an infinite increase in the numbers of those who would apply their minds to knowledge, now so few; being only the remainder of those whose fortunes give them leisure, after all, to whom

whom the same fortunes prove an avocation, are deducted.

We have now attained two ingredients, action and ease; which, (the third flowing spontaneously from them) according to Mr. Hume, constitute happiness. The former of these procures the subordinate requisites of human happiness. The labour of a father of a family, working a few hours daily on the land, would produce all the food necessary for its comfortable subsistence; and the industry of the other parts of the family would furnish what was necessary for their clothing, &c.; the few things which these would not yield, might be provided by certain persons that might be reserved from the manufacturers, who must be, in that case, sacrificed to the public good, and therefore should be as few as possible; and those should be requited amply for their submitting to such disadvantages, and be furnished with other gratifications, to counterbalance them. I know but of few things necessary to the most complete happiness, which any inhabited

inhabited country in the world might not in this manner furnish for itself. These few things are medicines, but these are in number very small, not exceeding half a score, or a few more. These articles, namely, the Peruvian bark, opium, quick-silver, brimstone, wine, &c. being almost the only articles in the Materia Medica that are deemed specifics, or that, perhaps, contain any healing virtues at all; the power of all the other drugs to do good being very doubtful, whilst their powers to do harm are very great *; a society therefore may be, without any great loss, deprived of them; and perhaps, considering the unskilful hands who generally use them, without any loss at all. Of these which we have mentioned, three only are of foreign growth, of which a few ships yearly would bring home, to any nation, the quantity required.

If it was thought proper to retain the

* This is also the opinion of Dr. Heberden, who seems to have taken the best method of ascertaining the real powers of medicine.

knowledge and practice of certain languages, arts, and sciences, a few men, whose geniuses for them were distinguishable, might be selected, and likewise sacrificed to the public good ; who should also be amply compensated, and in return be provided with necessaries from the surplus in individual hands : and as mankind would in general enjoy leisure, which would be employed by every person according to his inclinations and talents, there would be a much greater chance of obtaining men of great proficiency in every science than there is at present, out of the few that apply themselves to study of any kind. There are in few nations, in the present state of things, above ten or twelve thousand who apply to learning at all ; these are principally the clergy, in most civilized countries, of whom not one in many hundreds apply to any science, so as to make any improvement in it.

By this system, another advantage may be gained, which is superior to any consideration I have suggested ; indeed superior to any other consideration that can

can occur in human affairs, a blessing far greater than is to be found in the most opulent nation; I mean the certainty of the continuance of those necessaries and comforts of life.

In this state every man's land, the source of all his comforts, would be unalienable, he could not of course be deprived of it; and as his time would be so much superior to what is required to procure his daily and annual consumption, a stock for some years may be always on hand, effectually guarding against unfavourable seasons, or other accidents which might occasion a scarcity or famine; all famines, in almost every civilized country, being occasioned by the diverting too much of the labour of the people from producing and laying up a proper stock of provisions.

It is to be observed that, in most civilized countries, great stocks of all the other works or manufactures of the poor, such as the rich use, are provided and laid up; as is evident by the long credit the merchants and wholesale men can give: but with respect to corn and other necessary

necessary things, none is laid up; the reason of which seems to be, that the rich (the capitalists) are sure, in the worst of times, to procure enough for themselves; and it is to be feared they little regard what may happen to the poor.

This state of security is by no means to be found in the present state of civil society. No person, however high in the order of the rich, can be sure of the continuance of the possession of his wealth. Distresses, executions, imprisonments, show this daily. These are constantly before our eyes, and no human industry, care, or foresight, can prevent them. The poor indeed are exempt from them; they, alas! are already so low that they cannot sink lower. In this medium state, what a man had, would be little liable to be taken from him by another, all strife about *meum* and *tuum* would nearly be at an end. At present, as among brute animals, all war against all; so, in a civil state of mankind, all men contend against all men.

I shall say nothing relating to what the cause of virtue would in general gain by this change;

change; in which, on the one hand, people being relieved from their extreme want and ignorance, would be free from temptations to thieving and the grosser excessess; and in particular from the proneness to drunkenness, to which their poor diet now almost irresistibly drives them. And on the other hand, the rich would be exempt from the vices their great wealth exposes them to; especially from that worst of all vices—oppression of their fellow creatures.

It has been considered by divines, that man, in consequence of original sin, brought into the world a corrupt nature and wicked dispositions, which are the occasion of all the evils of mankind. It is true, that not all who have studied the Scriptures with equal attention and veneration, agree in deducing the same inference. For my part, who am inclined to draw effects and consequences from physical and moral causes, when these appear adequate to them, rather than from any other less suited to human understandings, I cannot help considering all, or almost all that which is called

called original corruption and evil disposition, to be the effects of the system of civilization; and particularly to that prominent feature of it, the great inequality of property. Do we not see in children artless simplicity, pure disinterestedness and benevolence, so constantly as to be characteristic of that age; and does not Scripture itself characterize children by those qualities, and, as such, declare them fit for the reception of the gospel*? As they advance in life, the natural dispositions of that age become gradually altered and corrupted I would ask whether any other cause whatever is so well adapted to counteract and destroy these good qualities of simplicity, disinterestedness, and benevolence, as the *mine* and *thine* established in such a rigorous and unrelenting manner? What so adapted to destroy the simplicity of children, as the art, the craft, the fraud, which their parents and all about them are perpetually, and, with regard to the bulk of mankind, necessarily prac-

* Monthly Review.

tising?

tising? What so effectually opposes disinterestedness, as the necessity they see, as soon as they can observe any thing, their parents are under of considering themselves only; and that, with all the attention to themselves only and to their wants, they are still so ill provided? A kind of self-defence and self-preservation renders it impossible for them to show an example of disinterestedness; for them to pay attention to that virtue, would be sheer folly. As to benevolence, they see few instances of it exercised on themselves, their parents, or neighbours; and they themselves having no means of doing acts of that kind, it must be seldom amongst their thoughts. I believe, as long as this system remains, divines may preach, and authors may write schemes of education, as means of planting those virtues amongst men, with very little effect, even if corresponding practice in themselves co-operated with their instructions.

## SECTION XXXVIII.

### WHETHER THE INDUCING AND KEEPING UP A MORE EQUAL STATE OF PROPERTY IS PRACTICABLE.

MANY able and good men have seen the evils attending the great inequality of property; but, not being aware that they were destructive to the degree that we have demonstrated them to be, they have suffered other considerations to overbalance them in their minds. All these considerations have been mentioned and discussed before, except that arising from the difficulty of reducing property to a level, and keeping it so. This has been asserted to be impracticable, and on this supposed impracticability are all the arguments against it founded; and on this alone all attempts to establish it have been reprobated.

Although the method recommended, for the removal of the evils in civilized states, was very short of a perfect equality

lity of property, it was not from a persuasion that it was impossible, but that it is not adviseable, let us, therefore, see whether it is as impracticable as it is asserted to be; and that with regard to England particularly.

In the following passages of Scripture, Deuteronomy chap. xv. Leviticus chap. xxv. verse 10. Joshua chap. xxii. verse 8.; it may be seen that the debts contracted by individuals of the Jewish nation were remitted, and ceased to be recoverable, every seven years; and that all landed estates, if alienated, returned to their former possessors, every Jubilee, which was every fiftieth year.

All such persons as believe in the Divine origin of this institution, will not only believe the fact, that such a regulation was established; but also acknowledge the wisdom and justice of such a law. And all other people must allow the fact to be founded on as good historical authority as can be produced, it being not only on that of the sacred writings, but also on that of the Jewish, Greek, and Roman historians, the law

and

and practice being continued down to their times.

From the above-mentioned passages, it may be inferred, in the first place, That an allotment of land was set out for every man, on the first institution of the state; and that, probably with few exceptions, the allotments were equal; that therefore a state of equality of property was established in a nation by God himself. 2dly, From the regulations that were to take place every seventh and fiftieth year, there would be very few rich, or very few poor men in it; and that therefore this state of equality would be permanent: for, since every man had a proportion of land equal to his support, none but the very improvident would incur debts; and if they did, as every man would be freed from them every seven years, it would be only the very improvident indeed that would be reduced to sell their land. And if any one person did bring himself to that necessity, every fiftieth year (which on an average would happen every twenty-five years from the time of the alienation), his land would be restored to him or his heirs; both of whom, as they must see the bad effects of his conduct, would be more cautious in future: and of course these temporary alienations of land would seldom happen.

Neither would there in this state be any number of rich men, and of course few able to purchase the allotments of other people; for, as originally, and at the end of every fifty years, none would possess more than one allotment, few surpluses of the necessaries of life would arise; which would be the only consideration that could induce the seller to sell, and also the only means that could enable the buyer to purchase; for, according to Josephus, in his book against Appion *, "The Jews were mere agricul-"turists, who subsisted on husbandry, and "tilling their ground, having no traffic "by sea, like the Phœnicians," &c. In countries where there are no manufactures or commerce, there is little other wealth but the land and the immediate produce of it.

From the whole history of the Jewish

* Joseph. contr. Appion, Lib. i.

nation,

nation, from the time of their first foundation as a state, till their dispersion under Vespasian, a term exceeding fifteen hundred years, a fact is ascertained which has been confidently denied, namely, the practicability of a system of equality of property, it being not only established in a numerous nation, but was more permanent, and that with a less departure from its original state, than any other system of polity that ever existed in any nation of the world ; and, as far as we can judge, with the best and happiest effect.

But it might be said, that in the instance of the Jewish nation, the land was originally parcelled out in equal shares before any other appropriation of it had taken place, which, therefore, was much more easily done, than it would be in case of making a new division of the land already divided, and in the firm possession of a part of the people, from whom great opposition might be expected. That this would be attended with difficulties must be allowed, but let us see whether the opinion of the absolute impracticability is well founded.

Mr. Eden has supposed that there are seventy-two millions of acres of land in England. If, then, the people amount to two millions of families, there would be an average of thirty-six acres for each family. This portion of land, greater or less, according to the size of the family, would most plentifully supply it with every thing that is wanted *. It would also supply labour for two horses or bullocks to work on the land; and would be a proper quantity to keep them employed; and with this quantity of land, the owner might procure a sufficiency for his own use, and wherewithal to barter for implements of husbandry, such as ploughs, harrows, carts, &c.

The distribution of land might be conducted in the manner following. The state, that is, the collected body of the people, might, as is natural, be possessed of all the land in the nation. By it, it might be parcelled out as above, and to

* This quantity of land would produce so much as to enable every family to live in such a manner, at least, as one having 150*l.* or 200*l.* a year now does, agreeably to what I have before supposed.

it might revert wholly on the extinction of any of the families, and in part on the decease of any of them. But if the number of families should increase, more allotments might be made, composed of parcels taken from the old ones, which would of course lessen in size as the number increased *

And this would be the whole of the business of first reducing, and afterwards keeping up, the equal state among men; for this alone would keep all other things sufficiently equal to prevent any of the present inconveniencies: and surely this is not impossible or impracticable †.

What is said of the difference of bodily

* For this purpose, the land might be occupied as open fields are; or moveable fences should be used.

† And this an abolition of the law of primogenitureship would soon effect. A gentleman possessing a landed estate of 1000*l.* per ann. has five children, boys and girls: to each of these he leaves 200*l.* per ann. or 200 acres. If we suppose these five children married, and to have five children each, the portion of each of this third generation would be 40 acres. But the land in this case would be kept in certain families. A law to prevent intermarriages of landed people would immediately disperse it among the whole of the inhabitants.—This method of reducing landed property has nothing violent or impracticable in it.

and

and mental abilities of different people, their different degrees of industry, &c. these would produce no other effects than that they, who were possessed of them, would be better supplied. It would have no effect in occasioning other men to be worse supplied; it would be creating no power that would be exercised over other people; whose unalienable allotments would render them perfectly independent of all other men; whose labour would be for ever free and under their own direction, and the whole of the fruits of which they and their families would enjoy---which surely would be the highest inducement to industry that could possibly be conceived: the supposed want of which in this state of equality is the principal objection made by Mr. Hume and Dr. Paley, and the only one they and others seem to rest on.

Some laws no doubt would be necessary in this simple state of matters; but they would be few, corresponding with its simplicity. If a father of a family, for instance, neglected the cultivation of his allotment, and by that neglect suffered his

family

family to be ill-supplied, he would be a just object of the law.

But how few would be the laws required here, in comparison with those of most civilized nations; which hardly any man of the brightest talents and of the greatest industry, and in the longest life, can make himself master of; and are therefore the occasion of so much misery to many people, in almost every civilized state. The simplifying of things seldom renders them more difficult. Whatever difficulties arise in the present political systems, proper remedies occur at the same time. In almost all states the laws of them are requiring alterations and amendments every day. Do we reject the use of a clock because it requires daily drawing up? We find that whatever restraints and impositions the governments in most civilized countries wish to lay on the people, they easily frame laws to accomplish them.

But it might be said, if this measure is so practicable, how happens it that it has so seldom been tried?

We have heard of three instances where an equality of property has been established;

blished; one among the Jews, another at Sparta, and a third under the government of the Jesuits in Paraquay. In all these cases, as far as we know, it was in a great degree successful. But it may be asked, why have we had no more instances of it? The cause has been, and continues to be, the avarice and rapacity of man. Until the state of unequal property was established, the evils attending it could not be known; no means therefore would be taken to prevent them. After it had existence, the existence itself would prevent all methods being used to remove it. Men, when they were in possession of wealth, and possessed also the power inherent in wealth, would of course employ this power, not to abolish, but to establish the wealth and power more strongly in their hands: an instance, therefore, where equality of property has been fully established, has rarely been seen.

But although we have had no great experience of the practicability and good effects of the state of equality among

people—

people—yet we have had more than sufficient experience of the bad effects of the state of inequality of property. On the side of the former we have had some experience which was in its favour---on the side of the latter our experience has been great, and greatly in disfavour of it.---To which side therefore does experience incline?

But if the prospect of any melioration of the state of mankind, from the obstacles and opposition in the way of it, may be impracticable and ideal; yet can it be said that the grievances complained of, are ideal? Are the causes of these grievances ideal? But if the grievances are real, if the causes of them are real, can a remedy, founded on these evils and their causes, be merely ideal?

## SECTION XXXIX.

### THAT THE PRODUCE OF LAND IS IN PROPORTION TO THE LABOUR BESTOWED ON IT.

In order to be convinced that the land is productive in proportion to the labour bestowed on it, and in particular with respect to England, we may consider that,

1st, In most civilized countries, about a third of the land lies in a state of nature; great part of which, if labour was bestowed on it, would be productive.

2dly, Of that which is cultivated, at least two-thirds are in grass, and not more than one-third under the plough.

3dly, That the ploughed land, which is the only land labour is bestowed on, and is not above one-fifth of the whole, produces more than all the rest: which will appear, if we consider,

That the whole of the wheat, barley, oats, beans, pease, potatoes, and almost all

all other vegetable food, which compose so great a part of the sustenance of the people, is the produce of the land in tillage. Moreover of the animal food, a great part of it is produced also by the same land; both with respect to the rearing and feeding. Throughout the kingdom in general, the year-old sheep, and all the fattening sheep, are kept on rape, turnips, cabbages, &c. during the whole of the winter, i. e. the whole of the scarce season; this is done by means of the great yield of an acre of turnips, &c. being not less than ten times that of grass in winter. Also a very great proportion of the summer-fattened are fed on the first year's clover; which is the immediate produce of the plough, and will carry three times as much stock as the natural grass. As to bullocks, all that are reared after the first year, when they have hay, are maintained on straw, with a few turnips, during the winter season; and a very great proportion of them fatted on turnips and grain in the same season; i. e. all that are fed for more than seven months in the year. Hogs also are almost wholly fed

on

on potatoes and grain. The chief part of the provender of horses also comes from the ploughed land, as well as their litter. Hence it is evident that the whole of the vegetable food of man, and at least one-half of the animal food, arise from the ploughed land. It is well known that vegetable food makes almost the whole sustenance of the poor; the great mass of the people. It furnishes the whole of their beverage. It furnishes the whole of their linen-clothing; and, by contributing so much to the support of sheep and cattle, it yields a great part of their woollen, clothes, leather, &c.

Thus it appears that a small part of the land furnishes the chief part of the sustenance of man, probably five-sixths of the whole, in the present state of things: the cause of which is, that more of the labour is bestowed on it than on other parts. It is obvious, therefore, that to increase the quantity of the sustenance, the method must be to increase the cause, which is the applying more of the labour of man to the land. This labour is employed on it,

1st, By manuring it. 2dly, By working it. And, 3dly, by destroying the weeds.

Providence has ordered that the remains of all animal and vegetable substances should become after death, by a natural process, namely, putrefaction, the means of promoting or keeping up the natural fertility of the land. And, as it seems that these are the only substances that have this effect, it is probable that if these substances were returned to it without diminution, and in a proper manner, they are fully equal to the purpose intended*. These matters, which are infinitely more valuable than the filings of gold and silver, which the workmen are so careful to preserve, are collected and restored to the soil in a very imperfect manner, for want of sufficient labour employed for that purpose.

Animal manure is composed either of the bodies of animals after death, or of the excrementitious parts that proceed from them during life.

Animals which might be converted to

* Lime is now known to be the produce of animals.

manure after death, are either human, or brute.

The former not only make a great part of the living creatures that are to be found in civilized countries; but a very great part of the other are consumed by them. By the custom therefore of burying their corpses deep in the earth, the surface of it is deprived of a very great quantity of the manure it would otherwise have.

The latter, i. e. brute species of animals, are principally, as we said before, consumed by the human species; so that there is but little of their carcasses returned to manure the earth; little care being usually taken to return the offal; as bones, blood, &c. to the ground. Of horses, asses, &c. which are consumed by dogs, and birds of prey, none can be said to be returned.

The other species of manure, namely, that proceeding from excrementitious matters of animals, compose the principal part of animal substances that are returned to the soil; of these however a very great part is wasted. The fæces and urine

urine of the human species, though containing the substance of the greater part of all other animals and a considerable part of vegetables, are returned to the land in a very small degree; and those of all other animals, in a manner that does not bring all the advantage to the land that it ought. The dung of cattle and of sheep, falling on the surface, is either in a great part washed away into the rivers by the rains, or left to evaporate by the wind and sun. The dung of neat cattle, falling in large parcels, does, probably, harm to the pastures, by making certain parts of them rank. The waste of manure is particularly great in cities and large towns, where the common-shores carry off almost all the refuse vegetable and animal substances.

All this appears, except the manner of disposing of the dead bodies of man, to be occasioned by the want of a sufficient quantity of labour bestowed in collecting those animal and vegetable remains, and applying them in the proper manner to the ground. The manufactures being thought to be

more

more productive of bread to the poor, than the richest manure: though it is probable that any given quantity of animal manure will increase the quantity of corn to many times it's own weight.

To preserve the manure, cattle should be kept and fed in houses, where the dung and urine should by all possible means be collected and preserved; for which purpose it should be put in places walled and covered. The fodder brought to the cattle would go much further. Both these advantages, in order to be obtained, require more labour. Large quantities of manure, both animal and vegetable, might be drawn from the sea; as well as lime, and earth to be burnt; the effects of which can never be lost; for any additional manure laid on the land produces an additional quantity of plants: and those plants when converted to manure, being returned to the land without waste, for ever keep up the increased fertility.

With respect to the working the soil, it is evident that it is of great importance that it should be done well. It is in general very imperfectly done, both with

regard

regard to depth, and to its being reduced to the proper degree of fineness. It is even thought improper to raise much mould, there being seldom sufficient means to enrich it: but if the quantity of dung is increased, we might avail ourselves of this better method.

The roots of all plants when young are tender and weak; and, in order to their penetrating through the earth, and spreading freely among it, require it to be soft and easily pervious; to a sufficient, that is, much greater than the usual, depth: and for this purpose it is necessary, not only that the ground should be well pulverized before the seed is sown, but that it should be kept so by hoeing, or otherwise, during the first stages of its growth. Rains falling after the seed is sown, on soils that have any clayey particles in them, dissolve the earth into a sort of half liquid or mortar, which being afterwards baked by the heat, frequently concretes into such a close and hard mass as greatly to prevent the spreading and growth of the roots, by which means the plant is stunted in its growth, and the yield of seed or corn much lessened.

If by accident a grain of wheat, barley, or oats, is dropt in a garden where the land is well and deeply worked, sufficiently, but not too richly manured, and afterwards kept clean and loose, with what vigor and richness does the plant grow; how many stalks does it throw up; and what quantity of seed produce! Every seed of wheat by proper culture may be made to produce some hundred-fold; by which, though it be an inferior consideration, much seed would be saved.

The destruction of useless plants or weeds is as essential to the growth of the useful plants, as either dung or the working the land; since the standing of one plant within a certain distance, hinders the thriving of another. But for want of labour in the extirpating of rooted weeds, and in the preventing the seeds of annuals and others from ripening in the fields and hedges, there are none of our field crops in which there are not plants peculiar to each soil, i. e. weeds, in far greater number probably than those composing the crop. This is seen among the crops when growing, and in the stubbles

bles after the crop is cut; where frequently the grass and other herbs are in such plenty as to afford the thickest and best pastures on the farm: but the detriment to the wheat, &c. must have been very great, and not to be compensated.

The chief difference between agriculture and gardening consists in the land being in the one worked with the plough, in the other with the spade; and in the means used afterwards to keep it from weeds, and loose. The latter method is in general used in Flanders. By this the ground is deeply worked, and the manure carefully buried, and secured from evaporation, or being washed away. The labour of doing this is great; but the produce is in proportion still greater.

In this way too the labour would be done by man to the exclusion of horses. In the present system, horses are made use of, in order that the men may be reserved for the refined manufactures. The reduction which this occasions, of the food of man, is great; one horse consuming as much as eight of the human species:

species: as is asserted by a writer in Scotland, who had opportunities of seeing it in that country, where the food of horses and men is the same, namely, oats. A saving in the consumption of the necessaries of life for the use of man, is the same as an increase of them in the production.

It appears, from the above premises, that one-third of the cultivated land, or one-fifth of the whole land of the nation, produces three-fourths or four-fifths of all the food, both animal and vegetable, for the whole people, even in the present state of cultivation; and this arable land is the land on which most labour is employed. If, therefore, the whole of the land was tilled, the produce would be at least three times the present quantity; and if the whole was cultivated in the best possible manner, as to manure, pulverizing the soil, keeping it clean and in a loose state; the quantity of the produce would not be calculable.

But it may be objected that all land is not fit for ploughing; and, 2dly, that the arable

arable land requires rest, by lying down five or six years.

As to the first, all land that is dry and sound, which all land is, or may be made so by skilfully draining it, would be more productive, if ploughed, than if it remained in grass; some strong and cold clays, watered, and other rich meadows, excepted.

As to the second objection, viz. that land requires rest by lying down in grass six or seven years, it is, I believe, a very unprofitable notion. The small quantity of grass which, after the first year, is yielded, besides the loss sustained by it, can carry little stock, by which only the land is enriched; for it is the animal matter received from them by the soil which enriches it. Well-informed farmers know how much better this intention is performed by proper successions of crops, i. e. the making a leguminous crop always succeed a culmiferous, and by carefully preserving the manure, working the land, &c.

As the only means by which the land

at present in tillage is kept in condition, is, by restoring to it the substances it has produced, in a putrefied state; and as by doing this in a more complete manner, a greater increase of the produce would be occasioned; so, by the same means, any additional quantity of land might be supported and kept in condition under tillage, especially if the other methods suggested were put in practice.

What is said on this subject shows, in general, the great increase of the produce of the land that might be obtained by applying more labour to it; and also suggests the method of doing it. What we have further to say tends to confirm what has been said, and also applies the method to practice, in the case of a single family.

We will suppose a man with a wife, and three children, all strong and healthy, as the employments and manner of living proposed would generally render them: this family we will also suppose, furnished with three acres and a half of land, of the average quality; and that it is also supplied with spades and mattocks of different

different breadths and sizes, a wheel-barrow, and the other usual tools of a labourer. That on this land, in the autumn, he puts half an acre of wheat in the ground, and a quarter of an acre of winter vetches. After which, during winter, he employs himself in digging with his mattock the rest of the land for his spring crops. Some time in the winter he sets out one-fourth of an acre of cabbage-plants, of the large kind. In the spring he sows three parts of an acre with vetches, clover, chicory, beet, parsley, lucerne, or any other productive vegetable, fit for summer fodder for hogs, cows, &c. He also sows one-half of an acre of barley, oats, pease, beans, Indian corn, or other grain, for feeding hogs, &c. and one-fourth of an acre of flax-seed. After this, one-half of an acre of potatoes. In the proper season he sows the remaining part of the land with turnips, ruta-baga, rape, Swedish turnips, or any other root or plant fit for the winter keep of his live stock.—The proportions of these crops may be varied. The putting in of all the crops, the season for doing which

coming

coming on successively, the quantities being what they are, and the man being furnished with mattocks of different sorts, (the use and forms of which are better known in Devonshire than in any other part) and with the occasional assistance of his wife and children, will easily be accomplished in a proper manner and time. A man with this tool, after the ground has been once ploughed, and the turf rotten, or breast-ploughed and burnt, will easily dig up, to the proper depth, one of the above-mentioned divisions in four or five days, for the first time in winter; and any subsequent ones in less time. All these crops should be put in rows or drills, or any other manner convenient for hoeing and hand-weeding. These operations, if the weeds are not suffered to grow high, and the ground hard, before the work is done, are performed with great dispatch; and the advantage of the crops being thus kept clean, and the ground loose, is very great. The taking in the produce, being also successive, is very easily managed.

With

With respect to the use or manner of consuming the produce, it is as follows: The wheat, which we will suppose to amount to fifteen bushels (it is generally a great deal more on land managed as proposed) the family eats; as many of the potatoes also are consumed by them as they stand in need of, the rest are given to the cow or hogs; as we suppose the peasant chooses to keep a cow and hogs. He may also keep ducks and fowls. The cow he supports in summer on the vetches, lucerne, &c.; in winter with the turnips, cabbages, &c. Late in the spring, and before the summer forage comes in, potatoes supply the interval; some sorts of them in Devonshire lasting very good till the new ones come. The cow, thus fed with succulent food all the year, will produce a great quantity of milk. By the means of the spare milk, and potatoes, and other both winter and summer provisions, some hogs are kept. By the use of potatoes and tail-wheat, &c. he maintains a considerable number of ducks and fowls; ducks indeed maintain themselves, chiefly, on worms, snails, &c. and are the most harmless and profitable animal that is kept.—The quantity that each of these divisions produces is fully equal to what is required of them. The half acre of potatoes will produce probably 120 bushels; what of those remain, after the family is supplied, will be equal to the keep of the cow, the interval between the turnips and vetches, which is short. Half of an acre of vetches, which may be mowed four times, is fully sufficient for the summer's keep of one cow and a hog, or two or more, according to their size; and the cabbages, turnips, &c. for them during winter, must be an ample supply. The family will have fifteen bushels at least, probably considerably more, of wheat, nearly enough for their whole support: six bushels being deemed sufficient for a grown person; as many potatoes as they can use; the milk, butter, or cheese, from the cow; the bacon of a hog or two, fed by potatoes and the barley or pease; some part of the barley for beer; also the carcass of the calf every year, and the flesh of the cow every five or six, or to share the part of one every year with their neighbours, if so agreed on.

To keep this patch of land in condition to bear crops, two methods are to be used; to alternate the culmiferous and leguminous crops, and to keep it perfectly clean from weeds, and with a minute attention to collect and convert into manure in the best manner all the produce that comes from the farm; for which purpose the cows and pigs must be kept in houses properly constructed for the different seasons, both in winter and summer. The dung containing all the vegetable and animal matter, carefully stratified, should be kept in a walled and covered place, and a floor of soil of a sufficient thickness laid in the cow-house, to receive the urine; which soil is to be dug up, when fully impregnated with it, taken out, and fresh brought in.

The woman, assisted by her children, and also by her husband, prepares the flax, spins and weaves it; which, in the coarse manner required, she easily learns to do. What things otherwise are wanted, and cannot be provided by the family,

may

may be procured by some of his surplus produce, by way of barter.

The cow might be made to plough the land, though that is not necessary, and harrow it; the former, with a proper plough, she could easily do in this well-worked land; the working her only a few hours a day would not hurt her milk, but benefit her by air and exercise. Mr. Bakewell worked the best of his cows and heifers. Horses should not be kept till we can get rid of the prejudice that prevails against eating them.

By this method, I presume, five persons may be supported comfortably on three acres and a half of land; that is, nearly a soul and a half to an acre: in which case, as there are in England 60 millions of acres of land capable of being cultivated, nearly 90 millions of people might be comfortably sustained, where nine-tenths of our present ten millions are pining. But whether I am strictly within the truth in this supposition or not, whether a little more or a little less than three acres and a half may be necessary, I am sufficiently near it to prove what I have asserted, viz. that

that the produce of land is proportionate to the labour bestowed on it, for this produce is much more than ten times as great as the present; and would be proportioned to the number of hands employed, if all the manufacturers, ten times doubled, were added. If an acre more was allowed, a second cow might be kept, which, with the other, would plough all the land *.

* The Earl of Lauderdale calculates that a farm, consisting of 504 statute acres, under the management which he directs, would produce sufficient for the support of one thousand nine hundred and seventy-seven people; and consequently that nine millions of people would require only 2,412,746 acres. In that case England would support 180 millions. This is on a wholly vegetable diet, which, I think, they ought not to be confined to. Many animals might be reared on the waste grain, potatoes, &c.

Dr. Anderson says, that in the richest land, the difference of produce from tillage and grass is in no case less than as three to one. In land of a middling quality, as ten to one; and in land of bad quality, when improved to its highest degree of productiveness, as one hundred to one.—See Dr. Anderson's Correspondence with General Washington.

The fertility of ground, in temperate regions, is capable of being improved to an extent which is unknown; much, however, beyond the state of improvement in any country of Europe.—Paley's Moral Philosophy, vol. ii. book vi. sect. xi.

APPEN-

# APPENDIX.

## Note A.

Dr. Colquhoun ſuppoſes that above twenty thouſand miſerable individuals in London, of various claſſes, riſe up every morning without knowing how, or by what means they are to be ſupported during the paſſing day; or where, in many caſes, they are to lodge the ſucceeding night.

To theſe pariſhes, Whitechapel and hamlets, the poor reſort, both from the nature of their employments and the impoſſibility of finding habitations any where elſe. They have, perhaps, no legal ſettlement where they reſide, or the funds of the pariſh can afford but a very ſcanty and inadequate relief.—Depreſſed with ſickneſs, and broke down and diſpirited by extreme poverty, the little furniture and apparel of man, woman, and child, is carried to the pawnbroker's, to obtain a ſcanty pittance for the immediate ſupport of life; until at

length

length there does not remain what is sufficient to cover their nakedness: In these miserable mansions, the author has himself frequently witnessed scenes of distress which would rend the heart of the most unfeeling of the human species.

P. Colquhoun's Treatise on the Police of the Metropolis.

In certain situations at sea, as in the cases of Captain Inglefield, Bligh, &c., and the crews of their boats, how do we compassionate them, when we read the narrative; and how do we burn to give them relief! We have many thousand instances in the metropolis, where the distress of the sufferers is not less, and who are equally unable to procure food; though in the midst of profusion and waste. About such, notwithstanding, we give ourselves very little concern.

## Note B.

The poorer sorts of society, in great towns, are peculiarly objects of commiseration: the wretchedness of their habitations, and the general appearance of distress and poverty, so often observed in them, form a striking contrast with the ease and

opulence

opulence of the higher ranks. The state in which so many of them live, however, goes further than barely the deprivation of comforts. From the confined, crowded nature of their habitations, contagion is generated and kept alive, and frequently diffuses its baneful influence far beyond the place of its origin.

The house contains as many families as rooms; and it is stated, on the authority of Dr. Willan, that from three to eight individuals often sleep in the same bed; no means are employed for ventilating the apartment; and, when any one family is attacked with fever, the wretched and perilous state of the whole can hardly be conceived, but by those who have an opportunity of witnessing it. The disease frequently spreads from room to room, till the whole neighbourhood have become subjects of its attack; and as no proper means are taken to remove the contagion from the walls and furniture of the habitation, a source of febrile infection often continues long, and it is to be feared never entirely disappears from the dwellings of the poor.

Remarks on the Poor of the Metropolis, by Dr. T. A. Murray.—Medical and Physical Journal, 1801, No. xxv.

## Note R.

From the many voyages of discovery that have been undertaken by different nations at such great expense; in which so many hardships have been endured, so many lives lost; from which so great expectations have been held; on which so great encomiums, as to the charity and public-spiritedness of them, have been bestowed—what benefit has been or can be received, either by the people, at whose expense they are undertaken, or by them who may be discovered in such voyages? The answer to this, which seems to satisfy every body, is, that they will extend trade and commerce; the value and advantage of which nobody disputes, but of which nobody has any thing more than a general idea. But we should descend more to particulars, and ask in what do these advantages, which they do or can bring us, consist? People do not consider that the whole of trade and commerce is contained in the exchange of the articles sent out and brought home—Now, what articles can be carried out? none, with respect to us, but the necessaries of life, as has been before demonstrated.—And from

from the people discovered, what can be had in their present state? nothing but some natural productions; almost the whole of which, except perhaps a non-descript plant or two, is furs; to all of which, in intrinsic value, the fleeces of sheep are much preferable—and if they are hereafter civilized, what can then be had, but works of art, of which we have too many already?

## Note W.

With respect to the rich farmer, some advantages accrue to the public from his riches, since by them he is enabled to make some improvements in his land, which poorer ones cannot: and no disadvantages arise from his riches, but those which flow from wealth in other persons' hands. A wealthy farmer may be considered in two lights; as a rich man and as a farmer: in the first character, he is an unprofitable consumer, and so far detrimental to a state: in the other, he is useful in proportion to his industry and knowledge. In the former, he is not more prejudicial than any other person of the same degree of wealth; in the latter, he is much more beneficial. The prejudice against

against them may possibly arise from their being supposed to have acquired their fortunes by taking advantage of the necessities of the poor, and principally by keeping back their corn from market: to this objection an answer has already been given.

We may add, that the wealth of a rich farmer may be supposed to have arisen from means that have been of advantage to the people; namely, from his good crops of corn, and other plentiful productions of his farm; for without these he could never have become rich; and these could not be, without greatly benefiting the people.

## Note K.

Some people, perhaps interested ones, are often heard to say things very different from these; as that the rich, by spending freely their fortunes, encourage trade, promote the circulation of money, &c. &c.; but if we examine this matter a little deeper, we ſhall diſcover the shallowness of these notions.

The rich do not spend their money without having some return; this return can be nothing that is not the produce of the labour of the poor. The return therefore may be called the labour of the poor. Now it is evident, the more labour of the poor is given to the rich, the less must remain to furnish the neceſſaries to the poor, and the necessaries and comforts to the middle sort of people; of course they can enjoy fewer of them.

We have seen that a man of 40,000 *l.* a year employs 1,600 men; a man of 80,000 *l.*, 3,200 men. There are said to have been, in France, some princes of the blood, and other nobility, who had, before the revolution, 800,000 *l.* per ann. they would therefore each employ 32,000 men. Every man who spends 1,000 *l.* per annum employs the labour of 40 men. The number of men that are required to furnish the families of the rich with such things as they consume, bears a very great proportion to those that remain to furnish necessaries to the poor, and necessaries and comforts to the middling class of people. It is plain, therefore, the former muſt be in a great degree destitute; and the latter very scantily supplied, that is, must be in very straitened circumstances. How different is this from the plenty said to be scattered by the rich!

In their houses, and immediately round them, profusion is seen; but for this profusion the people at great distances are pinched.

## Note L.

*Referring to page 45, line 24.*

It is said, things are always to be had, if there is money to buy them; and therefore there is really never a scarcity of provisions. This is a matter that requires explanation only to ill-informed minds.

We will suppose, at a time when wheat was scarce, and sold in the market at twenty shillings a bushel, that suddenly all the poor had their weekly pay doubled. The people, in that case, would be able to pay forty shillings a bushel; and as there would be a great competition, would pay, probably, that price; but would receive just the same quantity of wheat. No more wheat would be to be had on the account of there being more money. Again, if the pay of the people was suddenly reduced to half what it was, that half would purchase all the corn: the money that is in the hands of the people, be it more or less, will buy all the provisions in the market, except what is bought

bought up by the rich. In plentiful years, corn may be kept up for a year or two; but we speak of a number of years together; in which case, if it is not brought to market, what becomes of it? is it thrown into the rivers, or is it buried? Nothing occasions dearness but scarcity; and nothing occasions scarcity that is permanent, but there being too few hands employed in agriculture.

I say nothing with regard to exportation, for I do not confine myself to any one nation, but extend my view to most civilized countries that have any intercourse; where, if exportation takes place one year, importation does another.

## Note M.

*Referring to p.* 83, *l.* 18.

We perhaps may now see somewhat of the motives and principles of that practice, in some manufacturing kingdoms, of preventing manufacturers from leaving their country, by which means they are deprived of the greatest right of a free man, namely, to do the best he can for his own advantage,

The reason avowed is, that the manufactures are the support of the poor; and that by suffering the manufacturers to take them out of the kingdoms to which they belong, the remaining poor would be hurt. This is a presumption not sufficiently established to ground such a proceeding on. If it is true that manufactures are not the support of the poor, but have a directly opposite tendency, and that they are useful only to the rich, it would seem that this practice must be founded, not on public utility, and the good of the poor; but on an interested principle, to wit, the desire in the rich of retaining the poor man to labour for themselves.

## Note N.

*Referring to p. 149, l. 16.*

Rich persons are often heard to express a satisfaction at the increase of the cultivation of potatoes, considering it as a great resource to the poor. It is true that potatoes furnish the poor with a belly-full, which otherwise they might not have; for I believe there are few bellies full amongst the poor, but what are made so with potatoes. This, however, rather seems a matter of regret than of joy—that the great mass of mankind should be reduced to live so much on so poor and watery a diet;

diet; so unnatural to a carniverous animal as man is. It seems that the time is coming, and is near at hand, being the next degree of poverty to the present; when the poor of most civilized countries will be sunk so low, as to have no other sustenance than potatoes—in a great measure, already, in some; in which case the rich, i. e. the few, will consume the produce of nineteen parts out of twenty of the whole land, in most kingdoms, leaving only the one-twentieth part to produce potatoes for the whole sustenance of the poor of them.

## Note O.

*Referring to p. 96, l. 21.*

It was with great concern that I lately remarked, in an English periodical work, a suggestion of such a nature as I could not have expected to proceed from the human breast. The writer of it, after taking notice of the great increase of the poor-rates, expressed an apprehension that the poor would one day or other, and probably soon, become a very serious concern to the rich, and a much greater burden to them than all other imposts of the state; and would render their estates of little or no value. On this account it was proposed,

posed, that some means should be taken to prevent the evil. As it was supposed to arise from the increase of the people, the preventive method of course must be, as it was judged, such as would keep the population under, and within certain bounds. These bounds, it was conceived, should be that their number might be sufficient to administer to the rich, and no more—looking on the populace in the light that they did on working cattle; that is, that they were created to serve them, and for no other purpose. The specific means that were to be adopted to this effect were not declared.—This sentiment, I believe, though seldom avowed, is by no means rare, notwithstanding the inhuman nature of it. Whether I have discovered any other method in this work which the rich will be inclined to adopt, I know not; but my having shown them that they are already in a very ready and certain way of effecting the desired purpose, will save them some unnecessary trouble; which therefore deserves their thanks. I have also shown that the increase of the poor-rates does not arise from the increase of the number of the people, but from the increase of wealth, and in consequence of that, the increase of the refined

fined manufactures, and of the diminution which must follow in the production of the necessaries of life; for want of which the poor cannot provide for themselves, nor can they be in any other way well supplied, but by altering the system of property.

## Note C.

*Referring to p.* 83, *l.* 12.

It may be said, that tea and sugar, two articles so much used by the poor, are brought from places distant from Europe; but it is to be questioned, whether the poor's being supplied with these can be considered as an advantage, or the contrary. Tea is certainly in very general use; but sugar is by no means used so generally; very few of the poor, in many parts of the kingdom use it with their tea, not being able to afford it. The general use of the latter is chiefly owing to the poor not having it in their power to procure any thing better, such as milk, meat, broths, &c. It has too, besides being palatable, the same attractive quality that tobacco has: it is of a sedative nature, and takes off or lessens the disagreeable feelings of the stomach that poor and scanty diet occasions. It affords

affords very little nutriment, and it is to be regretted that so much of the poor people's money is laid out on it.

## Note P.

*Referring to p. 219, l. 19.*

We will suppose that on the suppression of any particular refined manufacture, the capitals used to carry them on, become unemployed. These capitals may be either large enough to produce an income equal to the expenses of the owner; or they may not. In the former case, the capitalist, if he declines further business, must do something with his money to produce the income. He must therefore place out the money in the hands of some persons who would pay an interest for it. To enable them to do that, they must employ it in some business. What kind of business can this be? Not the finer manufactures, for they are suppressed. It must be in some business which is increasing, and requires an increase of capital. This can only be farming or the coarse manufactures. These latter would be soon full, as they are got up with little labour, and require few hands; it must therefore be the former, which would take them in an almost

almost indefinite number; it having been demonstrated that the produce of the land would increase in proportion to the number of hands employed on it, till the whole has arrived at the most complete garden culture. This increased number of hands, the increased capitals of the farmers would enable them to employ.

With respect to the capital of any person who had been engaged in the suppressed manufacture, which might be too small to maintain its owner, it would become necessary for him to apply it either to the coarser manufactures, or to the farming business: but, as the former would soon be full, it must be employed on the latter, where there would be room for it. In this manner the capitals now employed in the finer manufactures would be turned over to agriculture.

But to this it might be objected, that many would invest their capitals in the funds, or in the purchase of lands. It is to be considered that the refined manufactures are the great source of expense, which, being cut off, great savings from the incomes arising from both these species of wealth would follow. This would remove the necessity for the proprietors of either to sell, and would induce and enable them to buy, if any was to be sold. This therefore would probably not only take from, but add much to, the capital to be employed on land.

As to the workmen, they must, in the same manner as the capitals, be removed from their former employments, either to the coarser kind of manufactures or to husbandry, where these transferred capitals will be sufficient to give employment.

By capital we understand the wealth with which any business is carried on. Wealth, according to our idea, is power over the labour of the poor. This power, therefore, can direct the labour of the manufacturer into any channel it pleases; which it does in this manner. A workman in the finer manufactures, having no employment in his former trade, applies first to the master of a coarser manufacture in the same line for work: for instance, a superfine broad-cloth weaver applies to a coarse broad-cloth maker for work, where he succeeds till the master is full of hands. He now can get no employment as a weaver; but the farmer still wants hands, and can pay them. To him therefore he must go.

This

This would so happen in the common course of things; but, if it did not, the poor laws in England would lead to it. When a poor man is out of work he applies to the overseer, who must find him employment; which he does, in most parts of England, by sending him round, under the name of a rounds-man or levy-man, to the farmers, who are obliged to employ him; and to take such a number as is proportioned to the land they hold. The master manufacturers, being low rated, take few.

## Note Q.

*Referring to p.* 106, *l.* 12.

In order to express the degree or measure of a person's wealth, we say, a man has one, two, or three hundred a year. It would express more directly the same thing if we said, a man commands the labour of ten, twenty, or a hundred men: and this latter method would more truly and justly represent the relations of men, with respect to one another, and designate the conditions of individual persons; the servile condition of the latter, and the assumed authority of the former, would be more evident, and the condition in general of the

different

different orders of men in civilized states would appear less disguised and concealed.

## Note T.

*Referring to p. 93, l. 21.*

Another division of property in the complicated state of civilized nations, may be made, viz. into corporeal and incorporeal. Of the first kind are all material substances, whether the raw produce of the earth, or such as have received the labour of man, on which mankind set a value, or which will be taken in exchange for, or command the labour of man. Of the latter sort, viz. incorporeal, may be the debts contracted, both on public and private accounts, as the public debts of nations, and those subsisting between poor and rich, and other individuals *. This incorporeal property is a power or a claim on the future labour of the poor; it is incorporeal, because it consists of nothing that has at present a material existence: but the things, the

* A mortgagee may be considered as the owner of part of the landed estate on which the debt lies. A creditor, that is, the person to whom another man of property owes any thing, may be considered as having a share in the debtor's personal property.

transfer

transfer of which gave rise to the claims, may have had an existence, and have been afterwards consumed, and of course have no present existence; but the power of the creditors, (as the holders of stock, &c.) over the future labour of the poor, survives them, and constitutes a real, though incorporeal, property. This explains the nature of several kinds of property of which we had before imperfect ideas. It is also perfectly conformable to our idea, that wealth of all kinds is power over the labour of man. The difference consists in this, that the one relates to the present, the other to a future time. The establishment of incorporeal property, whether devised for that purpose or not, multiplies the claims of the rich on the labour of the poor; and by creating a large artificial mass of wealth, and the distribution of it, increases the number of the rich, and consequently of an interested set of supporters of government, be that government what it may.

## Note Y.

*Referring to p. 273, l. 2.*

It is generally said, when speaking of the great inequality of mankind, that it always has been, and always will be so. This certainly is cutting the business very short; but it seems to me to deserve a little more consideration.

The inequality of property, and the difference of condition of men depending on it, in most civilized states, have their rise from two the most natural and powerful passions to be found in man; these are avarice and ambition: the one strongly tending to encroach on the *things* belonging to other men; the other to obtain authority and dominion over the *persons* of other men. Both these passions, as we said before, being natural and congenial to man, must of course be as ancient as man himself, and for the same reason must continue as long as man continues to exsit. But because these passions, and the injurious effects of them, have always existed, and are likely to do so, is that a reason why they ought to be encouraged or suffered? or is it not rather a reason why they ought to be resisted by all possible means?

As

As these two propensities in man may be stronger or weaker in different persons, so may they be accompanied with different degrees of powers, both mental and corporeal; and these different powers or faculties may enable the possessors of them to produce greater or lesser effects: and according therefore as these different degrees of the passions, and also of the powers accompanying them are great, so the resistance to be made to prevent their ill effects ought to be proportioned.

### Note Z.

*Referring to p. 105, l. 16.*

The rise of rents operates in a twofold manner in increasing the poverty of the poor; 1st, by the increase of rent the sum the proprietor of land has to spend is increased, by which means he is enabled to call off more of the labour of the poor from the employments that produce the necessaries of life for themselves, and of course to diminish them. 2dly, By the rise of rents, the sum the farmers are to pay being increased, they must of necessity, in order to raise that sum, set a higher price on the produce of their farms, the chief part of which is the necessaries of life. The poor, with the

the sum they have to lay out, can consequently purchase fewer of the necessaries of life; so that the scarcity of the necessaries of life, with respect to the poor, is increased by both means. 1st, By the rendering the quantity of them less in the market, which has always the effect of raising the price. 2dly, By the advanced price which the farmers put on them in order to pay their advanced rent. Nothing, therefore, can more directly or more strongly operate to the aggravation of the miseries of the poor than the rise of rents. We have shewn before, that the advance of wages never keeps pace with that rise.

---

## ADVERTISEMENT.

THE persons who may be disposed to criticise this work, will have an advantage, which no doubt will be made use of. Some of the opinions maintained in it being contrary to the more generally received notions, it was necessary to treat the subject in a somewhat elementary manner, beginning with the more simple matters, and such as were less contrary to the common ways of thinking, and proceeding to others more complex and more opposite to popular ideas. On which account, the Chapters in the advanced part of the discourse, if detached from their places, and exposed to view by themselves, without the preceding facts and reasons on which they are grounded, may appear paradoxical and untrue: The author therefore makes use of the right he has to put in his caveat against that mode of proceeding.

FINIS.

*The Author being at a distance from the Press, hopes to be excused for the following* ERRATA.

| Page | line | |
|---|---|---|
| 18 | 9, | *for* pars *read* pas |
| 32 | 17, | *after effect insert* (;) |
| 35 | 17, | *for* it *read* the world |
| 39 | 27, | *after* frequently *insert* of |
| 47 | 17, | *dele* as |
| — | 18, | *dele* thus |
| 52 | 24, | *after* as well as *read* into |
| 59 | 10, | *for* they *read* it |
| 70 | 6, | *for* sleling *read* selling |
| 89 | 5, | *for* guilt *read* gilt |
| 93 | | *dele* Vid. Note O. |
| 95 | 4, | *after* and *insert* of |
| 108 | 16, | *for* is *read* are |
| 119 | 19, | *for* near *read* nearly |
| 152, | | *dele* Vid. Note S. |
| 165 | 27, | *for* have seen *read* shall see |
| 170 | | *dele* Vid. Note R. |
| 172 | 6, | *after* but *insert* suffer |
| 190 | 5, | *instead of* their numbers is *read* are in number |
| 210 | 5, | *after people put* (,) |
| 212 | 8, | *for* to it *read* to them |
| 249 | 20, | *for* that *read* those |
| 256 | 26, | *for* as *read* that |
| 258 | 15, | *before* we *add* yet |
| 259 | 15, | *after* rest *dele* (,) |
| 260 | 16, | *for* which *read* whom |
| 285 | 15, | *after* woollen *dele* (,) |
| 286 | 26, | *after* lime *add* stone |
| 289 | 17, | *after* earth *dele* to. |

# OBSERVATIONS

ON THE

# PRINCIPAL CONCLUSION

IN

# *MR. MALTHUS'S ESSAY*

ON

# POPULATION.

---

BY CHARLES HALL, M. D.

---

*LONDON:*
PRINTED FOR THE AUTHOR,
AND SOLD BY T. OSTELL, 3, AVEMARIA-LANE; AND
C. CHAPPEL, PALL-MALL.

1805.
R. Wilks, Printer, Chancery-Lane.

# OBSERVATIONS,

## &c.

---

THE principal Conclusion in Mr. MALTHUS's Essay, being very different from that in my Essay on the Effects of Civilization, it seems incumbent on me to make some observations on it. Mr. Malthus agrees with me in many of my positions, and most of my premises. In particular he thinks with me, that the great scarcity of the necessaries of life, and the evils attending it, are occasioned by the employment of the poor in manufactures, instead of the land; but notwithstanding this, he does not consider civilization as chargeable with any thing on this account, because, as he says, the same want and misery must necessarily happen in every system, and particularly in a state of equality of property;

for

for as the number of the people would increaſe more than the ſubſiſtence would be made to increaſe, their number would ſo much exceed the ſupply the land would afford, whatever the culture of it might be, as, after ſome interval, to produce a ſcarcity equal to the preſent in civilized ſtates.

Mr. Malthus, though he allows, as we before ſaid, that all the miſeries above-mentioned, and the conſequent loſs of ſo many lives, are brought on the people by civilization; yet he not only thinks it not injurious on that account, but conſiders it as beneficial to them, and that for another reaſon beſides that above-mentioned; namely, becauſe it furniſhes them with a check to the increaſe of the number of the people, and by that means proportions it, as he imagines, to the territory they poſſeſs. Theſe checks Mr. Malthus explains to be of two kinds, the one preventive, and the other poſitive. Of the former kind is, the rendering marriages leſs frequent; of the latter is, the actual deſtruction of the people by want and miſery.

With regard to the rapid increaſe of the people, and

and the difficulty of raiſing the ſuſtenance equal to the number as it increaſes, it appears that I was not ignorant of it by what I have ſaid in page 258 of my Eſſay:—

"It muſt happen in the courſe of time, that the "whole world, and every part of it, will be fully "peopled; and that the produce of it will be inſuf-"ficient for the ſupport of the inhabitants, how-"ever well-cultivated it may be; but this period "muſt be very remote, and the event cannot be "prevented by any human means; are we there-"fore to anticipate the evil by any ſyſtem or prac-"tice of our own?"

The reaſon why I then took only a general notice of the poſſible arrival of this ſtate, ſome time or other, is,

1st.—Becauſe I ſuppoſe that in any caſe the period of its arrival is very diſtant; even although no preventive methods were uſed.

2dly.—Becauſe I ſuppoſe that by preventive me-thods

thods it may be removed to a much more diſtant period, even with regard to the whole world; and with reſpect to any given nation, that it might be prevented altogether.

3dly.—Becauſe I ſuppoſe, that, if ever it does happen in a ſtate of equality, it will not be attended with evils in any proportion equal to the preſent.

4thly.—Becauſe I ſuppoſe a part of a nation, eſpecially a ſmall part of it, to have no right to induce a ſtate of want, diſeaſe, and mortality, on the other parts of it, exempting itſelf at the ſame time from them.

As to the firſt ſuppoſition. I have shown, that, with a very imperfect cultivation, three acres and an half of land will ſupport five people *. It may, therefore, be allowed, that, with the perfect culture now ſuppoſed, namely, when ſo great a number of hands are employed on it, every acre of land, one

* Vide page 286.

with another, will ſupport two perſons; conſequently England (to make uſe of it as an inſtance on the preſent occaſion) will ſupport one hundred and forty millions * : an interval, therefore, of plenty, or a reprieve from ſcarcity and other evils, would be obtained till the people roſe to that number; which (ſuppoſing them to double every twenty years) would be nearly eighty years. But as plenty would only come on gradually after the change, and the increaſe of the people would not be immediately commenſurate even to that, on account of the many deaths that would be occaſioned in conſequence of the hardſhips the people had endured, we may lay the reprieve at one hundred years. Here then is a ſuſpenſion of all the evils, as well as an introduction of all the happineſs and comforts ſtated in my former work, to ſeventy millions of people, (the half of one hundred and forty, which is the average number if taken for the whole time

* In this caſe there will be one man, his wife, and three children, to cultivate every two acres of land nearly. Whereas, in the other caſe, the ſame people had three acres and an half to work on.

of

of one hundred years *.) Such a bleſſing, I maintain, as no human invention ever brought on mankind ſince the creation of the world. All other improvements bring ſingle advantages; this comprehends all advantages—extending to all people. Nor is the term it is ſuppoſed to continue to be deſpiſed. A term of one hundred years would cover our children, grand-children, great-grand-children, and great-great-grand-children, in moſt caſes. There are few meaſures, beneficial ones at leaſt, of any ſtateſman, which have ſo long a continuance. But—

As to the ſecond ſuppoſition. I have thought that this period might be protracted to a much greater length, if preventive methods were made uſe of. The principal methods of prevention are, colonization, and the regulation of marriages. The former was had recourſe to by the ancient Grecians. Whenever they were full, they ſent out colonies to the neighbouring iſlands, the coaſts of Aſia, the Cherſoneſus, &c. This is the natural method. Inſtinct directs many ſpecies of animals to do it. It is di-

* Wars, if any happened, would prolong this interval.

rected by the Creator of mankind himſelf—"Go," ſays God, "increaſe, and ſpread over the land." Colonization ſhould commence long before the people had arrived at the perfect culture of the land. To this uſe (the only good uſe it can be applied to) ſhould be devoted the whole ſhipping of a nation *. And this is the only caſe where colo-

* In 1803, the British registered shipping amounted to 21,445. The tonnage of them was 2,238,249. If we suppose that a ship will carry a man to a ton, one-fourth of these ships would carry, in one short voyage, viz. to Nova Scotia, a number of people equal to the whole supposed annual increase, even if it was as great as that in America: or if the ships made three voyages in a year, one-twelfth of the ships, exclusive of vessels of war, would perform it. And is our shipping rather to be employed in bringing home luxuries, than in preventing the allowed evils of civilization? It appears, therefore, that the prevention of the evils of civilization is absolutely within our power; and of course the argument built on the contrary supposition falls to the ground. In a state of equality we suppose foreign commerce almost to cease, the shipping would of course cease also: but the building of these vessels for this purpose only, would be no great burthen to a great nation. As 155,000 seamen, navigate at present all our shipping, about 12,000 only would be required. The fisheries on the coast, if properly encouraged, would bring up a much greater number. Mr. Malthus's treating, therefore, colonization as impracticable, is without reason.

nization

nization is juſtifiable; namely, when one country, being too full of inhabitants, (notwithſtanding all poſſible means had been uſed, or were uſing, to raiſe ſubſiſtence) ſends out its ſupernumerary people to a country not fully stocked with mankind; as is the caſe with a vaſt proportion of the globe. If the voluntary emigrations were not ſufficient, the deficiency ſhould be made up by compulſion, determining by lot who ſhould go. To fill all the world, even if all the nations of Europe ſhould adopt the plan of colonization, would take many generations, after they had arrived at a real ſuper-population at home; but if only one, or a few of them did it, the time it would take might be conſidered as without end. And this perpetuity of happineſs and plenty, whether it would be or not in the power of all the nations in the world to obtain it, would certainly be in the power of any given nation. Are we not to attempt a thing which we might ſucceed in, becauſe if all others were to do the ſame they could not all ſucceed? Is a farmer to be deterred from ſowing any particular grain, as barley, for inſtance, because all others might ſow barley, and the market thus be overſtocked?

ſtocked? Or, is the merchant not to import any particular kind of merchandiſe, becauſe all other merchants might, if they choſe it, do the ſame; and by that means exceed the demand? There are other preventive methods that might be adopted, without waiting for the dire neceſſity exiſting in civilized nations* Marriage may be regulated by law, and made leſs frequent, ſo as effectually to anſwer the purpoſe, without its being the dreadful conſequence, and urged by the deſtruction of millions, as it is in civilized countries. This regulation of marriage it might be impoſſible to obtain in the civilized ſtate of a nation; the rich there, who *only* have the power of making laws to enforce it, not undergoing the ſame hardſhips which the reſt of the people do, and which render the reſtraint neceſſary; but, on the contrary, reaping great advantages from thoſe

* It seems to me that the preventive method or check proposed by Mr. Malthus, is in effect the same as the positive check, or at least that they must necessarily be co-existing: for no considerable check on marriage could take place, except occasioned by the pressure of want and disease. The preventive method is the actual disease.

Sero medicina paratur.

very

very hardſhips, will never be prevailed on to ſubmit to it. But in the natural ſtate of over-population, if ſuch ever ſhould be, this, or any other remedy, would eaſily be applied; for every man being then in the ſame ſtate, every man affected in the ſame manner by the exiſting circumſtances, every man is equally intereſted, and equally inclined to ſubmit to any ordinances, wiſely calculated to remove the common evil. The conſtant claſhing of intereſts of the rich and poor in the preſent ſtate, (that of the former almoſt always reſiſting the general good and advantage,) will in this ſtate be done away, and this change will eſſentially benefit the condition of the people, if they ever ſhould become too numerous for the extent of their territory. With reſpect to England, colonization alone would be ſufficient to effect all that was required; and as to the world at large, where colonization could not so eaſily take place, (but it would always take place was it not for the intereſted views of the rulers of thoſe ſtates *) the reſtraints on marriage, by law, would be ſufficient. And it would never be neceſſary to deſtroy the peo-

* An instance of this is, the prevention of artificers from leaving their native country.

ple by want and the manufactures, as it now is in European ſtates; or by the expoſition of children, as in China: the latter uſage, however, I think infinitely leſs cruel of the two; in the one caſe the pain is momentary, and without any previous dread of it; in the other caſe, in order to be deſtroyed, the people muſt be expoſed to a long courſe of ſufferings, and, at length, after a greater or leſs number of years, they ſink under long waſting and painful diſeaſes.

As to the third ſuppoſition. I have imagined that, if ever, by the neglect of preventive means, this ſupra-population ſhould obtain in a ſtate of equality, it will not be attended with evils in any proportion equal to the preſent.

This condition of mankind, if it happened in ſuch a nation, might be conſidered as induced by nature itſelf, or, which is nearly the ſame thing, would be brought on by mankind following the dictates of nature: whereas the preſent is the effect of the artifice, injuſtice, and violence of man. Now we know that every thing that neceſſarily

and

and inevitably happens, is submitted to with much less pain than what is brought on us by man. We acquiesce in the all-ruling dispensations of Providence, when we know they are such, with much less repugnance, and they occasion less uneasiness. Further, the effects of natural supra-population would be borne by all alike. Every man s allowance, as in a besieged town, would be the same. All would share the burthen, and of course each man's share would be lightened. Whereas now the allowance of the rich, though these are in number no more than about the eighth part of the people, is eight times greater than that of all the others. In this state there would be no invidious distinctions, which add to the sufferings of the over-burthened; no degradation, no debasement, no contempt, no insults. If the people were hungry, naked, and diseased, they would not see others possessing, in infinite abundance, the means of satisfying their hunger, of covering their nakedness, and remedying their diseases. They would not see persons so superior to themselves in knowledge that they could hardly consider themselves of the same order of creatures; but must think themselves as overlooked by their Creator,—as the outcaſts of the earth. If they were ſtinted in the neceſſaries of life, they would not be obliged to labour any further than was neceſſary to produce thoſe they would have, to which therefore they would cheerfully ſubmit. They would be free from all the unwholeſome and ha eful manufactures. They will enjoy conſiderable leiſure, and by that means acquire knowledge. They would not experience that debaſement of the mind of man the preſent ſyſtem occaſions. If they ſhould be under reſtraint as to marriage, they will not at the ſame time ſuffer the hardſhips that are the effects of the full indulgence of it, as they now do.

In my laſt ſuppoſition, I have preſumed that a part of the people, and eſpecially the ſmaller part, cannot have a right to induce a ſtate of miſery and mortality on the great body of the nation.

If the effects of the ſyſtem of civilization are the direct and conſtant cauſe of the loſs of the lives of ſo many people, and that in a manner which is attended with the greateſt ſufferings, what human

power

power has a right to eſtabliſh or ſupport ſuch a ſyſtem? If the rich have a right, by the preſent degree of luxury, &c. to deſtroy the people they now deſtroy, in order to keep the reſt down to their preſent numbers; they may introduce a ſtill greater quantity of luxuries, and that to an indefinite degree, and ſo deſtroy and reduce mankind to any number, *ad libitum*. It is allowed that there is at preſent, and that there always has been ſince civilization has taken place, land ſufficient, if more labour had been beſtowed on it, to furniſh neceſſaries of life to its inhabitants, and of courſe to have prevented this loſs of lives; civilization, therefore, is chargeable with anticipating, at leaſt, the evils, and bringing them on the people, long before they would otherwiſe have been afflicted with them; and conſequently has been the occaſion of the deſtruction of all thoſe that have hitherto been deſtroyed by this cauſe. If by bringing thoſe evils on them, thoſe evils were rendered lighter than if they had been ſuffered to come on at their own time, (as that deſtructive diſeaſe the ſmall-pox is made milder by inoculation,) ſomething might be ſaid in behalf of it; but this reaſon or pretence is not offered. The

keeping

keeping the maſs of the people down can only be effected in the preſent ſtate by bringing ſcarcity, want, and diſeaſe on them; and theſe muſt be in ſuch a degree as to deſtroy (a policy ſhocking to think of) as many of the people as is neceſſary to prevent them from riſing above the number required; and of courſe the artificial want muſt be in ſuch degree at leaſt as the natural apprehended want; elſe it would not produce the effect deſired. The former ſtate muſt always be a miſerable one, and admitting of no mitigation.

Mr. Malthus in his Eſſay has the following paſſages:

"*To this end I should propose a regulation to be made, declaring, that no child born from any marriage taking place after the expiration of a year from the date of the law; and no illegitimate child born two years from the same date, should ever be entitled to parish assistance.—After the public notice, which I have proposed, had been given, to the punishment of nature he should be left; the punishment of severe want: all parish assistance should be rigidly denied*

*nied him. He should be taught that the laws of nature had doomed him and his family to starve; that he had no claim on society for the smallest portion of food; that if he and his family were saved from suffering the utmost extremities of hunger, he would owe it to the pity of some kind benefactor, to whom he ought to be bound by the strongest ties of gratitude.*"

The treatment of this labouring man, I cannot help ſaying, appears to me not only inhuman to the laſt degree, but unjuſt and iniquitous. I will aſk, why is he thus treated? Becauſe, it will be anſwered, he does not produce by his labour ſufficient to maintain his family.—But, I ſay he produces ſix or eight times as much as his family conſumes or requires, but which is taken from him by thoſe who produce nothing. What he is entitled to is, all that his hands have made or produced, the whole fruits of his labour, not that pittance his wages enable him to purchaſe. That he has produced what I aſſert, is literally true if he is an huſbandman; and, if he is an artificer, the labour which he applies in his trade, would, if it was ſuffered to be employed

on

on the land, do the ſame. It is not true that he has *doomed himself*, or that nature has doomed *him, and his family, to starve*; that cruel doom is brought on him by the rich. If any are to be treated in this cruel manner, it is thoſe who have been rich, and who have never produced any part of all they have conſumed. But none ought to receive ſuch hard uſage. The poor labourer is to receive no aſſiſtance from others, becauſe, it will be ſaid, by ſo doing he would be a burthen on the rich. I ſay he is no burthen on the rich; and that, inſtead of receiving any thing from them, he gives them ſeven parts out of eight of what he produces. He is under no ties of gratitude to them; and if he had ſenſations of an oppoſite kind, it might hardly be wondered at * Are the bees who produce the honey

* When the Germans, after they had conquered the Britons, took from them their lands and stock (which was all they had) in order to keep them in a permanent state of subjection; can it be thought the Britons considered themselves as under any great *ties* of gratitude on receiving just what was sufficient to keep them alive?—This very state of the victors and vanquished exists at this day: it is the same that at present is seen in the

honey under obligation to the drones for eating it? Are the bees a burthen to the drones, and not the drones to the bees?—But who are the poor men that are to wait before they marry, and to what time are they to wait? I anſwer, that not this or that individual, but none of the labourers, or any of the common mechanics, can rear a family, without the greater part of them periſhing for want, even with the intereſt of all the money they can poſſibly ſave during the time they remain ſingle.—Are they therefore never to marry? Are not thoſe rather to remain ſingle who do nothing to ſupport themſelves or the children they may have? And for whoſe benefit are the poor to remain ſingle, to be abſtemious and continent? For thoſe, I ſay,

the rich and poor: the one are the successors of the Saxons, the other of the Britons; it is an actual continuation of the same state. The two orders in it bear just the same relation to each other. The state retains all its essential qualities, altered indeed in appearance, and disguised by civilization, which throws the veil, that the use of money and manufactures furnish, over it; but in no degree does it lesson the servility, want, and misery of the system.

It is right sometimes to call the insolence and arrogance of wealth back to its origin.

who

who wallow in waſte and luxury, ſenſuality and luſt. No reſtraint can be juſtly imposed on any, unleſs they receive all the advantages to be derived from it. Theſe are the arguments that ought to be refuted by the Anti-vandaliſts, but by them they are wholly avoided. They muſt allow all this to be true when applied to the preſent time, and to continue to be true until the earth can, by no means poſſible, be made to produce ſufficient for its inhabitants. The rapid tendency there is in all animals to increaſe is evident; and that the increaſe has been kept down in all the nations of Europe, by deſtroying in various manners the young of the human ſpecies, is alſo evident to every the moſt curſory obſerver.—Mr. Malthus has travelled, it ſeems, over Europe, to evince the truth of theſe obſervations: for my part, I think that when I employed two or three pages in proving them, I did more than was neceſſary. But to prove that all theſe means, by which the maſs of the people are kept down, are juſt and neceſſary at the preſent time, this would require great labour indeed. The queſtion at iſſue is, Whether an evil, that may invade mankind at a diſtant period, in certain poſſible

ble contingencies, and in different degrees of ſeverity, and which may then be much mitigated, and even wholly removed, can be juſtly brought on the preſent generation in its utmoſt degree of force and malignity, in order to exempt a few from it, and by which exemption they are rendered capable and ſtrongly diſpoſed to add greatly to the evil? This is the queſtion,—it demands an anſwer*.

With reſpect to Mr. Malthus's opinion, that the want and miſery brought on mankind by civilization,

* I would ask, How comes it that the rich are so regardful of future generations in this instance, so contrary to their usual mode. They have entailed a heavy debt on posterity. In the one case they throw all the burthen, which they think will fall on remote posterity, on the present generation. In the other they throw the burthen, which the present generation has occasioned, on posterity. What then should be the occasion of this different conduct? I answer, their own interest is consulted in both cases; in the former they enjoy the effects of it; they enjoy almost all the fruits of the labour of the poor; they reap advantages from their wants and misery. They are benefited by bringing the difficulties, which may possibly happen in a future age, on the present generation.

tion, are not injurious to the people, becaufe by them their number is leffened, fo, he imagines, as to be kept within proper bounds; it feems that this effect it has, is confidered by him as a remedy to the evil, and that both of a preventive and pofitive, or, as a phyfician would fay, of a curative nature. On this occafion Mr. Malthus feems to have reafoned inaccurately. This ftate of want and mifery muft have arrived and attained to its full height, or, nearly fo, before it would have the effect of deftroying a fufficient number of the people, i. e. fome hundreds of thoufands annually in a nation of no great fize: It therefore is the difeafe itfelf, and of no fmall magnitude, and can hardly be thought a pofitive remedy. Neither can it, till its arrival, and till it has rifen to the degree mentioned, act as a preventive remedy; fince it is the feeing the dreadful effects of it that deters young people from marrying: it is therefore the difeafe itfelf, not a preventive check or remedy. What has happened cannot be faid to be prevented.

But further: I think I may be warranted in faying, that it is abfolutely impoffible, in a ftate of inequa-

lity

lity of property, by any checks, or by any means whatsoever, to regulate the numbers of the people, so that there ſhall be ſufficient ſuſtenance for the inhabitants; and I aſſert, that the condition of the poor in ſuch a ſtate can never receive any amendment; and that it muſt always be a ſtate of want and miſery. To whatever number the people may be reduced to in a civilized ſtate, ſuppoſe to one half of the former number, that number would be ſtill as much too great as ever it was for the quantity of ſuſtenance the country would produce. The matter is, not what the land might be made to produce, but what it would be ſuffered to produce: as is the caſe at preſent; it does not yield what it might be made to yield, but what it is permitted to yield. We have before demonſtrated, that wealth is power over the labour of the poor; and that the rich can direct their labour in any line they pleaſe. If the labouring people were reduced to half their number, the ſame ſmall proportion of theſe labouring people would (in caſe the ſame ſtate of property be continued) be employed to raiſe the neceſſaries of life for the whole; and the ſame great proportion would be employed

in

in the manufactures that is at present: the same cause would remain, the same effect would follow: the relative numbers of hands in each employment would be the same: and of course the same relative quantity of sustenance produced; consequently the same want to the poor; the same profusion to the rich. Hence we have said truly, that a remedy for the evils of civilization is in a state of civilization absolutely unattainable. Effective checks can only be applied in a state of equality of property.

I have often in my Essay and these Observations adverted to the difference between the produce of the land as it now is, when so small a part of the labouring hands are applied to it; and that which it would be if the hands now employed in the refined manufactures were added to them. It seems to me that Mr. Malthus, for want of making this just and necessary distinction, suffers an error to run through a great part of his reasoning and conclusions, and the practices he recommends pursuant to them. If the produce of the land was now what it would be, if so many hands were not drawn off from working on it by the power of wealth, many

of

of his poſitions would be true, which now are utterly deſtitute of foundation and truth. Mr. Malthus ſometimes, however, argues on the contrary ſuppoſition, as when he allows that the ſcarcity of the neceſſaries of life are occaſioned by the employment of the poor in manufactures inſtead of the land; and ſpeaks in favour of the check to the increaſe of the people occaſioned by it. But in general Mr. Malthus argues on the ſuppoſition of the want of ſubſiſtence, equal to the number of the people, as being inevitable. He otherwiſe would not think of reducing the number of the people to the quantum of ſubſiſtence, inſtead of increaſing the quantum of ſubſiſtence, and make it equal to the number of the people. This taking a fact in two different lights occaſions an inconſiſtency in ſome of his reaſonings, and error in ſome of his concluſions: it is an error to ſay that a man ſhould be doomed to ſtarve, when plenty of food might be raiſed; and when the labour of that man does actually produce great plenty in compariſon to what he conſumes; and when all others might do the ſame.

To conclude. Mr. Malthus's reaſoning drawn from the

the tendency of the people to increaſe in number in a greater proportion than their poſſible ſupply of ſuſtenance can be made to do, ſeems, for the foregoing reaſons, to be an inſufficient juſtification and defence of the unjuſt, cruel, and deſtructive ſyſtem eſtabliſhed in civilized nations; and that it will operate as an encouragement to thoſe, who were too much before inclined to oppreſs, to puſh their tyranny ſtill farther—But I am very far from thinking this was the deſign of the author.

And, therefore, notwithſtanding the argument has been ſet forth with all poſſible advantages, it ſtill appears that a more equal diſtribution of land would be an adequate remedy for the evils of civilization; and that it is the only one, and conſequently ought to be promoted by all who have a regard to juſtice, or compaſſion on the ſufferings of mankind. If ever we, both great and little, are called on for our real and unfeigned opinions, it is on this occaſion,

Hoc opus hoc studium parvi properemus et ampli,
Si patriæ volumus, si nobis vivere chari.

THE END.